Selected Poems

OTHER WORKS BY DENNIS SAMPSON

The Double Genesis

Forgiveness

Constant Longing

Needlegrass

For my Father Falling Asleep at Saint Mary's Hospital

Within the Shadow of a Man

The Lunatic in the Trees

SELECTED POEMS

DENNIS SAMPSON

Homestead Lighthouse Press
Grants Pass, Oregon

Copyright © Dennis Sampson, 2019. All rights reserved. No part of this book may be reproduced or transmitted in any form without the prior written permission of the publisher.

Library of Congress Cataloging-in-Publication Data
    Names: Sampson, Dennis, 1949-author.
    Title: Selected Poems / Dennis Sampson.
    Description: Homestead Lighthouse Press. Grants Pass, OR Homestead Lighthouse Press, 2019

ISBN 978-1-950475-01-8
Library of Congress Control Number: 2019937808

    Homestead Lighthouse Press
    1668 NE Foothill Boulevard
    Unit A
    Grants Pass, OR 97526
    www.homesteadlighthousepress.com

Distributed by Homestead Lighthouse Press, Amazon.com, Barnes & Noble

Cover art: Rembrandt

Homestead Lighthouse Press gratefully acknowledges the generous support of its readers and patrons.

Design by Ray Rhamey

SELECTED POEMS

Contents

Reverence for Life	1
Falling Star	4
from THE DOUBLE GENESIS	5
Cellars	6
Bat	8
Morning Ceremony	10
Falling in Love with Laundry	12
Bite Down on the Azalea	13
New Light	16
Prayer	19
Mornings My Uncle Couldn't Work, He Would	20
Meditation on a Typographical Error	22
from FORGIVENESS	25
I Wish I Knew Another Name for God	26
Making A Graveyard	28
.22	31
Forgiveness	33
Getting Fired	36
Father	39
Past the Remaining Animals	40
Before the Movie Begins	42
Looking at the Elephant Over My Shoulder	44
Need	48
The Commandment	52

from CONSTANT LONGING	58
Evening Inventory	59
The Snapping Turtle at Templeton Pond	61
Laundry in Venice	63
What Is Written Down	72
Blue Photograph	74
Pig Iron	76
Reading Habits	80
Devotional	81
Litany	83
The Leopard	86
The Anaconda	88
Shadows	91
Original Pleasure	94
In the Light of My Lamp	96
from NEEDLEGRASS	98
For the Dawn	99
Midnight of the Word	101
Eden	104
April Snow	107
What the Rising of the Dead Shall Mean	109
History	122
from FOR MY FATHER FALLING ASLEEP AT SAINT MARY'S HOSPITAL	124
the night the comet finally slipped into view	125

i see now, but i really can't say	126
death, that old complaint	127
black widow, in the predawn	128
a cricket kept me up all night	129
shadows in forsyth cemetery I pass this morning	130
the apple tree in november twilight can sleep now	132
a doe draws slowly out with its head up	134
look, I don't say to my father	136
come said the night, and I will fold my wings around you	138
in the silence the young indian orderly danaught	139
there is a cold god	140
i have always wanted to begin	142
in fall I hear the cry	143
for the coming of winter under the hunter	145
sing to me. i don't have the strength	147
from WITHIN THE SHADOW OF A MAN	148
Short Story	149
Creed	151
Mandelstam	153
To a Fly Along the Nose of the Generalissimo	154
Alone with the 23rd Psalm	156
The Noses of Old Men	158
Barnum & Bailey	163
Another Dawn	164
Wrightsville Beach at Night	166
Within the Shadow of a Man	167
Living Alone	169

from THE LUNATIC IN THE TREES	171
Solitary Cooking	172
The Lunatic Lies Down Under the Moon	173
Eating Emerson	174
How It Happens	175
The Lunatic and the Sun	177
The Lunatic at Prayer	179
The Lunatic Considers the Universe	180
Ant	181
On the Streets of Honolulu	183
Trinity	186
The Eternal Day	187
September Elegy for My Mother	190
Pet Shop	192
Getting the Christmas Tree to Leave	194
Clarinet	195
Missouri	197
Little Dipper	199
Why Men Don't Write About Their Wives	199
from THE DOUBLE GENESIS	200
Serpens Nebula	201
About the Author	202

For Larry Hamlin
and in memory of Phil Levine

*Then I forget my own trees
at evening moving in the day's
last heat like the children
of the wind, I forget the hunger
for food, for belief, for love,
I forget the fear of death,
the fear of living,
I forget my brother, my name,
my own life. I have risen.
Somewhere I am a god.
Somewhere I am a holy
object. Somewhere I am.*

Reverence for Life

  Polished on Saturday evening till they
glimmered
    beside the sofa for all of us
to see, my father's shoes
    seemed mystical to me,

    and after everyone had gone
  to bed I'd pick one up
and breathe the deep aroma
    of leather buffed and glowing

    then stare inside the mouth
  smelling of Dr. Scholl's
as if the secret of my father's being
    would be revealed. Kicked off

    at dusk they'd hit the linoleum
  with a thump and lay apart
barring their grey soles,
    finding their way back to stand

    like bride and groom in the closet,
  the tennis shoes and boots,
the wing tips accumulating dust

waiting for the day
when they'd be taken out
and given one more chance,
so much riding on their willingness
to fit and be beautiful!

Peering from underneath
the coverlet, trailing their laces
unraveled with a single
flick, or propped up

on the coffee table after supper,
they seemed so human,
encouraging one another to endure.
And when my father drew

me off his room to offer
for display the shoes
he wanted me to choose from,
each obediently silent and in

formation, I understood too well
what they had been through
and where their allegiance lay,
backing away from this family

I adored for never once complaining
and that I at first refused
to separate. In pain
I picked, at his insistence,

    the pair he hadn't worn in years,
  putting them up on my desk
to look at for the longest time
    as if the mystery of this man

    I knew so little of and who
  walked everywhere and never
threw a single shoe away
    would suddenly come clear,

    then crept back up the stairs
  and slid them into place
beside the others
    in this improbable cathedral

    of shirts and suits
  scented with cologne, with a gentleness
I would come to understand
    as reverence for the only life I had.

FALLING STAR

It was midnight. What I had written down
was almost finished and the revision
of cutting every one of the adjectives but "laughable"
seemed complete, leaving me to type the final draft

and lay it out neatly on the table,
a relevant gift to myself the following morning.
What was it that I saw flashing across the cosmos,
dying out just before entering the unconscious?

It had been years since I'd seen a falling star
and I remembered the moment. I was holding hands
with Ann on a night when the constellations were emphatic.
"That's Orion" I said and she said "Did you see that?"

I was caught off guard by this little reverie of mine
and rose from my chair, glad to be looking forward
to my words organized in four quatrains.
And that I had spent my life writing poems.

FROM
THE DOUBLE GENESIS

Cellars

Cold, dark, deliberately aloof,
they guard their solitude like great
ailing grandfathers. Suffering
nightly the chronic angers of huge
ill-tempered children, drafts through flues,
they, too, are equally inconsolable.

Imagine the vast preponderant webs,
the cricket, caught up in a fissure with its
cry. Imagine the constant longing.
They are like Kierkegaard
or Kafka, for while they do not appear
to prosper, their brooding is a prelude

to revelation. They are squat and dank.
Drawn upon by someone singularly alone,
the refrigerator spits and hums
through the dark ages of this gloomy room.
The spider hesitates in its web.

Shedding light on the dark
interior of this mind, somebody has flung
back the door, radiance in the wake
of something human! The cellar holds its breath.

When they have left, leaving
the big undulating light-bulb on

over the door, brooding resumes. Cobwebs reel
from the rafters, gusted by wind
through dim windows. Prayer,
repeated by some repentant poltergeist,
begins again. *Capoom.* The furnace kicks on.

BAT

    You are not all animal,
half animal, half stinking little demon.
Flaunting your tiny detestable face
to the photographer,
you flee through the winding labyrinth.
Can it be you soul
we see, quick
beyond calculation?
Anyone, I think, would call you cruel,
capable of compassion only at the last moment.
But agony in life makes you
less grateful. You do not know your name.
Bat, in the beginning
you were the one didn't wait for creation,
ill-digested, unpitying,
too far ahead for God
to call you back. You inhabited the original canyon
with your kind; only
at midnight did you loop and soar
far from the light
so as not to actually see each other.
How could you have continued with any innocence
having witnessed
that stark, disfigured face?

This can be said
to your credit:
I don't think you'd consent to death.
You are too stupid. Too inhuman.
Your face gives you away.
And I have seen you flutter and veer
like a kite, in a room of light,
half-panicky
to find a corner and die.
I have lifted you with a stick
and thrust you out.
You ascend anyway, being demon,
back to your cave.
Your kind doesn't recognize your presence.
They don't know you.
By instinct breeding, clutching, eating,
you grow old.
Everything they say about you is true.
You navigate gracefully.

Morning Ceremony

After dark I like to drive
down to Cross Creek
which runs under Morgan's bridge,
stopping, at last,
to get out and walk
the short path up to the lake
where I see two herons
waiting in reeds. Necks bent,
they walk, light-footed,
not noticing that I've
come up to watch
the half-moon bright
on their backs. At first
they look likely
to lift and fly
before I walk toward them.
Exactly as I pass
they point their beaks
above the hill,
but stay. No stars.
Struck by the coming light
of morning,
the sky lets down its moon.
I wait, then,

but they just bow,
one leg rigid,
the other, as if in penance, lifted.
It is first light,
not them,
that labors to explain,
streaking the lake and shadow.
They look as if they long to be alone forever,
bright blue, trembling
with dawn-shine,
unseen by anyone but me.
When they stroke
up from earth, outstretching their wings,
I see their beaks
lit up with sunlight
of my heart's want,
which is small, but which is rising
and rising till they are gone.

Falling in Love with Laundry

I love to look at laundry in late autumn,
long underwear, sailing against the breeze,
blouses and dresses, dripping with wet,
and those big baggy overalls, fading light to blue,
negligently left out under the stars all night.
And I love to come up to the towels and plunge my face
deep into their odor of water and air,
swept dry by the wandering breeze of the Dakotas.
I am one who understands the beauty of threadbare socks.
So I lean out to look at one woman, slender and small,
who stretches to pin her underwear up to the line,
flexing her neck, cleansed by an evening breeze
billowing up under skirt exposing her thigh.
Oh I shall go on praising the beauty of long underwear
and blouses rippling and flowing all through the day,
exuding their elemental freshness and color.

Bite Down on the Azalea

is what my friend said
when I referred to the flowers
by the house,
to the azalea tufted
with snow. Married still
at dawn to the faith
I associate with flowers
fooled by winter, it looked
so full it might
be eaten. The blossoms
altogether formed a kind
of heart, and the hue
and cry of the paired cardinals
above the fading frost
praised the azalea
for beauty and the sorrow
that was human. I sensed
a questioning in wind blown
briefly through wet leaves,
as if to say, *We share the human
mood; there are
no permanent truths.* Hardly
a moment had passed
when I surmised the foolishness

in thinking humans
less beautiful, less deceived,
and nature similarly immune
to lack of reverence
for this immortal world. We, too,
had wept the ancient glamour
into a face, and Babel
was *citte dolente*
to the visitor from space
who would not fault the azalea
from blooming. But finally
I tired of analyzing
the azalea, which,
having survived, shuddering up from the ground,
now adored the light.
I didn't eat the azalea.
And I cannot say
I had risen and understood
the importance of immortal beauty
in the light of this,
yet I know the truth can be cruel.
A man "depressed for weeks"
blew his jaw off
in a house not far from here.
The blossoms of the azalea
fall upon the ground
and flutter into a cloud
as if for the first time
and forever

they had wished to say,
Check your scorn (I did, directly),
for man needs help from every creature born.

New Light

Take this apple
into your hand, Anton.
Take it.
Luckily for us
two hands could hardly be
more beautiful,
especially since
the apple, wet with dew,
approximates
their solitary longing.
Abducted from the monk
who does not pray,
they say you would regret
not having touched
its suppleness of color.
It is a gift
from those who wish to see
your hands
held gladly out
close round this element of red.
Take this flower
into your hand, Anton.
See, it is ringed,
radiant as the apple

on the sill,
sated, wet with dew.
How nicely it shines
open to the grove,
cleansed in evening light.
We felt, because you love
this yellow color
you would be in agreement.
Tonight, by dark,
you might find solace
in its radiance.
Anton, if we
could be of help to you, we'd say
New light
on what you do,
this flower on the table.
Take this death
into your life, Anton.
Take it.
Not, by dawn,
will you revere
the light beyond the meadow,
nor clearly see
how gradually the apple
on the sill,
sated, wet with dew,
turns golden.
Dappled, like the flower
on the table,

it withers softly on your palm.
Perhaps, at dawn,
you will be kind enough to pray
for those
half out of love.

Prayer

I would like to sprawl in fury over the earth,
to purify the vile with a cast of my hand
and lie down in the pasture like light,
the grasses moving and broad
under my tremendous belly.
I would like to walk out of my body,
become another thing more muscular,
a huge mare brooding, solitary and brown,
beneath vast sky, her last life flying behind her,
becoming wind exploring with interest the winter trees.
I would like to glide beside these
high stacks of wood, trailing a finger
along the lip of a trough,
feeling the incalculable power of the land.

Mornings My Uncle Couldn't Work, He Would

rise up in rage,
and from somewhere around the house,
hearing the howl of snow,
wrench the inexpensive whiskey down
then drag a chair
before the picture window where
hour after hour he would watch
lights being struck in other homes
until my older sister told
ghost stories across the dark,
making us forget him,
and then to hear him hurl, not long after dawn,
the almost empty bottle
where it knocked and spun
and spat the whiskey out,
making him momentarily happy,
listening to him climb
the attic ladder,
where his last wife's letters were,
mumbling something
to himself, falling
backward on the ladder
and saying the hell with it. We

tightened when he cursed the air,
the ground he walked on,
and goldfish oblivious in their bowl,
so we locked the door
until the racket finally died
then went reluctantly up the stairs.
Sometime, later in the day,
he would rise again, quiet and remote.
That made us happy,
and we forgave him everything.

Meditation on a Typographical Error

(for Mark Jarman)

No *n,* and we have heave. I hear the word
As if for the first time and think of it,
Perfect to approximate the soul's escape
From the body, as better than heaven. Here
Is a star, heaven's glitter, garish
With the sky's stellar brightness,
Heaved from the hand of the Maker

In the beginning, when there was nothing.
Heaven, uninvented. It was heave
Before heaven, before people, before the word,
Heave, beleaguered by the earth's emptiness, by stillness,
The heave of matter, and the heave of life
In the organism, the heave which brought
The first creature, ignorant, from the water.

I like the word, yet am terrified
By its violence. Heave; as when the mother screams
And yields to the fetus in her belly,
Heave of the wind, the martyr heaved into the flames
After an hour in the sun
With others, who, sick at the thought,
Retched black gruel upon the ground. Heaven

Is hardly imaginable. But heave,
Unholy as the stone held and heaved at the heels of
The heretic, heave is the product of the body's
Difficult knowledge, Adam heaved from paradise
And Christ, familiar with heaven, heaving the cross
Up the hill, jeered at, then himself nailed
To the cross and the cross heaved into position

With his body on it. Lucifer heaved
From heaven, who now delights in the heave
Of souls into hell, created when our earth
Heaved to make way for him,
Repulsed. But it so happens heave
Is equally beautiful as heaven, two words
Unlike in meaning, yet separated by a letter. For isn't

The meteor heaved through the night sky
Memorable to the lovers, the water heaved
From the precipice the point in putting
Hands above our eyes to watch
Beside the waterfall? The man on his deathbed
Heaves forward, to face his family,
Before he suddenly knows the secret heaven

Keeps from us; the egret crouches and heaves
From the cypress, flowing low over the lake,
Then heaves himself beneath the rippled surface
And is gone from the eye, heaving himself then
Up with tremendous power. Heave.

It does not redeem like its lovely counterpart.
But it is vivid. It is always with us. Not heaven, heave.

FROM FORGIVENESS

I Wish I Knew Another Name for God

    I wanted to speak
    about the spider
    between the daffodil
    and daylily,

    not the black widow,
    not the daddy long-leg,
    but that fat garden spider
    stopped between flowers,

    a spider
    speckled white,
    big enough to eat a luna moth.

    I wanted to speak
    about the spider,
    seeing the blue-bonnet wasps
    copulating on the screened-
    in porch,
    bringing my eyes
    so close
    it must have seemed indecent
    to the god of wasps

and all other gods

the god of spiders
the god of gravel
the god of wind-blown trash.

Making A Graveyard

They were making a graveyard. First, they took hold of the earth
   with those huge yellow caterpillars I was afraid of

when I was a child. They groped, and shoved the deep black loam

while the men in white hardhats stood and talked under the only shade
   tree there was for miles. At noon, the drivers climbed down

out of the cabs and sat next to each other, the wisps of cellophane

      blown up into the air and the thermos bottles shooting

      a glimmer of light
      just as they were hit by the sun. They looked ill-at-ease,

getting up to piss or just mopping their brows, cracking jokes about
   somebody else's girlfriend. I knew I could never go back to that
even if I had to. They broke up right on time, although one

lay face down in the dirt, asleep, until he heard
   the desolate engines start up and he got up and went back to work

like the others. They heaped the boulders off to one side,

then flattened the earth, running for cover before the thunderstorms
   broke, grasping their caps, while the wind picked up enough to rattle

the plywood shelter they had built for themselves. Pretty soon

     the graveyard took shape,

     you could divine it. No lumber anywhere,
     no forklifts, and the swaggering workers staying longer
                                               each day

taking fewer breaks. They brought in trees, evergreens I think,
   to get a jump on the headstones. Done,

     it looked like an island,
     fastidiously designed, with a picket fence

and a caretaker, wavering in the haze, who clipped
   the hedge and never looked at his watch, sitting up

in his pick-up while the ministers shouted their prayers. The funerals,
one right after the other, were beautiful to behold,
   especially when the casket, quivering with new snow,

made its way painstakingly over the graveyard grass.

     The gravestones grew in great number. By the time
     it was spring
     the marquee with special rates appeared

>   beside the highway,
>   "We deal intelligently with the dead."

And I had to ask
why I had come to love the sight of so many gravestones
and not be haunted by the mourners

laying down bouquets and wreaths on the graves.
Can you see a child buried and ever forget it?

In June, the caretaker comes and goes through the wrought-iron gate.
The sprinkler whirls.

.22

You took the .22 out of your father's closet
one morning to polish the barrel with a cloth,
first the inside, glittering when you gazed
down the long eye held up to a window,
then the dark-brown stock, nicked and scratched,
that loved the pressure of your cheek when you brought
a magpie down in the grove above your house,
a flutter of black wings collapsing through
branches without a sound. From a clump of
strawberry blossoms, the scared eye stared back
at you and you left it there, too afraid
to put it out of its misery.

Laid out on the table, shining, the .22
had a curious beauty. It tempted you,
although you knew it was empty.
You checked the chamber again and again
before squeezing the trigger, then put it back
in the closet with your father's suits
and wing-tipped shoes, where it remains,
unused for two decades by either of you.

If you went back to that house you would find it
fallen along the wall, the bolt swung open

and chamber caked with dust, and copper bullets
scattered in a small wooden box in the basement,
with antiquated keys and nickels and pennies.
In privacy you would do it all over,
polishing the barrel with the soft cloth
and placing the .22 on the table
where it would wait for you,
as if ablaze,
like one of the dead present and burning everywhere
and all at once in the mind of a child
ready to be lifted up out of his grave at last.

Forgiveness

My father came home drunk and was dazed
by my mother's rage in the driveway,
driven back into shadows by her hand

while all the neighbors slowly turned
to their mowers in the dusk and their garages
shedding light on the lawns still spinning with sprinklers.

I had never seen him so quiet before,
holding carnations in his fist
as she answered her own questions and called

him inconsiderate for coming home so late,
forgetting their dinner date and dance
at the VFW. And when I thought

she had finally stopped, striding toward the door,
I saw her make the mistake
of praying, arms uplifted to a starless night,

that she be delivered from a sonofabitch.
He turned, no longer apologetic,
flinging the bouquet straight in the air.

They did not live together after that
for nearly a day, deliberately alone
in the farthest corner of the house,

my sisters and I conspiring to bring them together.
That night, alone in my own room, half asleep,
the full moon looming in my window,

I felt the hallway light on my face
when my father opened the door
and opened my eyes, seeing him strip to his underwear

and get in bed, saying *Give me some of the covers.*
I could have begged him to go away
and let me sleep, needling him

until he mumbled for me to shut up
but I stuck it out. When I woke
his side of the bed was empty, the blanket

whipped back, for he had gotten up in the dawn.
I lay there in the light, awhile serene,
then sat beside him on the davenport

while he moped, not looking at my mother
singing vindictively at the sink
with suds up to her elbow.

Taking my mother's damp hand
and leading her to the figure just as dazed
as when she raved in his face the night before,

my sisters on the other side, insistent,
forcing her to sit in silence beside him
until he gently touched her and they forgave,

I realized that I could survive my father
sleeping beside me through the night
although I only wanted to be left alone,

seeing them together once again,
my mother ashamed, my father blushing,
having no other alternative but to embrace.

Getting Fired

That night after getting fired I sat
in the living-room and waited for my father to get through

his disgust – pacing, pacing – waited for him to find his way

past accusations I was lazy and never lifted
a hand – a smartass

that lipped off and couldn't look adults in the eyes –
waited for the shame

when something so delicate is touched
it will never be the same, like the baby

magpies I caressed high in a maple
only to learn later

their mothers hated the scent of human flesh…
waited for the pain we name fatherhood,

we name strength,
to dissipate and be replaced by grace

of a hand set down firmly on the upper bone of the shoulder,
that fellowship that comes of being enemies

and now friends...
and I waited for the silence after the ultimatum

so searing it made me wince,
when everything is reconstructed again.

When a father finds out a son is fired
on Friday because he did not understand

the difference between a plumb bob and a compass,
taking all the rage of a stranger

in the middle of a construction lot in May,
is not the father supposed to show mercy

and seek to console, opening his past
to an anecdote about his greatest humiliation,

a slap by somebody he loved
to tease, changing the way he looked at the pitiful?

But my father wanted me to fight back that night,
like a child

flailing in the midst of his torturers at recess,
wanted me to resolutely defend,

raising my face to his face without saying anything
and one of us backed down

and both of us were changed.
Trailing two daughters up the walk,

peace was restored by the appearance of an angel
the following day. I was ashamed

while my father had shown
the power of humility was immense when he stepped back,

silent beyond all saying.

FATHER

My father hated tomatoes and only swore once,
when I touched his upright sole above the covers.
It was the love of a child, without thought,
that blew a stupendous bubble over his head
one summer and watched it wobble and slide,
slicker than a womb, till he reached up
and pressed it with his forefinger and thumb.
Thirty years have passed since that bubble popped.

If time exists at all it exists in the mind
of an angel so degraded she could bathe for days
without being clean, without being cauterized. I'd like to find
my father again and say that simple name
that signifies obedience to someone wiser.
"Father," I would say, not to apologize,
"do you remember the time…" and he would nod,
remembering every trick I pulled as a child.

Past the Remaining Animals

The animals do not want us,
flying or pacing or just at rest.
Why does the gorilla
vomit into its palm,
the monkey grab its cock?
Only the gazelle is still,
a study in apprehension.
Shame on the lions
shitting in front of women,
and languid bear
licking a pallid loin.
Shame on the baboon
that peeks at its hands
like a human being and screams.
I want the dangerous dream
of a leopard in the dark
and escape of zebra,
not dung
in the dungeon of rhinoceros
and hippo. Then
I come into a silent room
where the spectator
does not speak,
seeing the slow cobra

coil and uncoil
until it is comfortable.
And I remember every
curve, every crevice,
along that monastery floor
closing my eyes,
opening them to the cobra
alone in another corner,
and clairvoyant.
This is the horror
we have been waiting for
and take with us
past the remaining animals.

Before the Movie Begins

The light is dimmed and something like love
comes over every one of us, the kids
off to my right calming to a whisper and a couple
close to death (they must be in their eighties)
helping each other with their coats,
then sitting silently before the movie begins;
but there is awhile still for light
conversation and even mild applause
when a can is kicked over and descends
this hillside of cement facing the screen;
time for the late-comers that flood the seats
with light near the door to stumble one
behind the other down the aisle
and the attendant to reprimand a teenager
for shrieking, steering his beam of light in her eyes.

See how the arm is lifted at last
alongside the neck of another,
how the head of a woman leans
and the failures of everyone are forgiven
with a hand that caresses the hair of a man
unhappy with his life; a family
passes popcorn back and forth
while somebody shows a wristwatch

to the screen to see how much time we have.
There is the girlfriend glad for the first time
since the dance, when the one
around whom she has constructed her future
fell into the arms of the first-to-ask;
there are the brother and sister in the front
dropped off by their parents and scarcely visible.

What is this sudden kinship that I feel
with the people in this half-empty theatre,
not only the old couple closing
the wrapper on their candy so they won't be tempted,
the children too, and horde of adolescents
grooming themselves in the darkness
that diminishes the longer we all sit here?
Who will be the martyr? Who will grieve?
Who will discover love at the end of a long
and mystifying life and die in peace?
Somebody changes seats and their fate
is altered… or they remain the same;
the curtain parts and we prepare
(a child touched to silence, an anonymous *shissh*)
for what is coming, and does not come.
And we see each other completely in the light.

Looking at the Elephant Over My Shoulder

Just another June day and then an elephant
appears through the windshield of my car. How strange,
how absolutely marvelous
this huge sauntering hump being led around a ring
on the lawn of Jack's fast-food restaurant
for promotional purposes no doubt,
although what possible analogy could there be
with an elephant wrapped in a blanket
that says ELMO in large white letters?

I arrive in the almost religious
ecstasy of being in the presence of an elephant,
fathers coaxing shy daughters into the care
of the handler who ushers them up the movable stairs
and, with gentleness, lifts and sets them down
on the broad back. This is happiness
for even those on the highway,
their faces struck with wonder…

   One night, in bed,
borne aloft in dreams and feeling
     just elation
      (I was getting away from my ex-wife)
   I woke to a woman
        all in white

*below the ceiling, shimmering
in candle-light. "From heaven, as you name it
    (we have no designation), I've been asked
to appear.
       So here I am.
Is this sufficient for you to change your ways?"*

"Beatrice," I cried.

*"No, Doris, done with living.
I will not haunt you with the truth
  but only say
you got it wrong. Patience is the way."*

    *Was she
  the angel that fought so long
with Jacob?*

      An elephant
so tolerant of strangers, so morose,
rocking primordial as the ocean.
I have to suppress my impulse to pay whatever it is worth
to feel the backbone of a god walking
between my thighs. After rides
the introspective elephant turns away
his baleful head, tugging at the rope,
hind leg lifted slightly, and he seems
on the verge of sleep. What must he think?
Does he dismiss his suffering
with, *Forgive them, they know not what they do?*

When she had gone, I lay
  my head
on the pillow, chalking it up to booze,
    determined
  to stay off the liquor for a while.

Out of nowhere, again she came, enraged.
   "Death will be miserable.
  You ought to be afraid."

  Praying throughout the night, next to my bed
   she stayed.
I joined her in my pyjamas.

A child, close to slipping, her eyes wide, clutches the tough hide.
The sun is low
over the treeline, cars come from the dramatic show of love
for the one who says nothing at all,
who does as he is told
with the flick of a stick against his quivering flank.

Another child, nearly toppled by shifting shoulder-bones,
shrieks and clings to the delicate scarf of hair
as Elmo pauses – indifferent to the awe of everyone.

    At dawn,
  she fled. I saw this spirit rising in the air.
     She said, "Go back
  to the daffodil you spotted on the path,

breathe deeply,
enough to catch the scent.
Look in the heavens. Aren't they frightening?"

"Don't get too close,"
a mother warns, then glides her palm along him
as he passes. No one notices. I stare,
then steer apart, looking at the elephant over my shoulder.

Need

> "Mercy has many arms."
> – Roethke

I watched two women make love once
when I lived in Iowa City
and the wind and snow blew
in January like the absence of mercy.
While two women I knew embraced
on a mattress
in candle-light flowering above their heads,
I stood outside a window
with the uneasiness of a man about to take a vow,
my hands in my pockets,
glancing around
into a world without any innocence,
the brunette whose sweetness I had tasted
looking through her long legs
while her lover drank deeply
spreading the thighs wider by pressing gently
with her open hands,
the woman I had come to love letting her face
fall away so her hair
pooled on the floor and her tongue
licked over her lips

and she lay with her palms up
and arched her back,
saying something I could not hear
from my sanctuary of wind,
a phrase that might have forever changed me.
I watched, closer to the pane
scarred by ice
that let me see
until euphoria shook Elizabeth loose
and they lay apart
in the flow of the candles,
too sated to move. I believe they might have seen me
if I had blinked,
since both with half-closed eyes gazed out into the night.
When the light from the house behind me
shed its vastness over the snow
I vanished
through bare branches leaving tracks
they would find later
when a neighbor pointed out
the need to be more careful,
to draw the blinds and never go out alone.
I believe they would have named me
with a sickening hiss,
allowing me to flee like cellophane blown wildly
across the street, reconsidering every kindness used to define men.
And I think they would have crucified me
with silence
and I would have had to justify my eyes
to Elizabeth who had softly touched my face.

All I could think of was that negligee
lifted over the breasts
and legs that did not resist the parting hands,
all I wanted to recall
was the tongue feasting on flesh so pure
it was appalling.
Lying awake that night in my apartment
I whispered to the stranger I had created,
who called on me
to go back over every moment of what I saw.
I knew what I was doing
when they worried over foot-prints the following day
and image of a hand
on the window where I fed my emptiness,
afraid of being caught.
I gave in easily,
not knowing if the shudder that swept over me
was inspired by wind
or desire
so deep I could have cried out,
crashing my fist through the window
as they slid from the scent
of the bed
to the hardwood floor and fumblingly rose,
touching
each other with a tenderness reserved for strangers.

I told no one what I saw.
In February
with wind blistering my face and my fingers aching

I came to a church
named after an angel and waited wildly in the nave,
watching the flames
of the candelabra accentuate the craving
of one about to suffocate, his eyes
shut down as if ashamed,
so emaciated
I thought I heard the outcry of his bones
beginning to break
and I escaped
before the priest put something on my tongue.

Now, nearing my house that can't be seen
from the highway, I notice
the leaves of the hickory beginning to change.
It is dark in the living room and all I see
is my daughter's aquarium through the door,
fish I watch when I am tired,
black mollies, angelfish
lifting their long fins in the heated water.

I should remember them for their sensual
choreography.

How considerate they are
of one another's need to drift
without interference,
not even flinching when I press
my hand to the glass,
lightly rising and gliding off to the side.

The Commandment

Sometimes driving home from the library at night
I take the long way leading out of town

past Buttermilk road and the paper mill
where there is one light on and the nightwatchman

between rounds stares through a golden cubicle,
his back to the moon rising on summer nights

so he can see each vehicle on the highway. On evenings
when the stock-car races let out and a stream of lights

can be seen for over a mile, he must go crazy hoping
one will turn at the gate and girls emerge

insolently waving and flaunting their slender beauty
in the headlight's glare, perhaps a can of beer

flung end over end at him from the driver's side
as they screech away and he diligently records

this incident without criticizing the world.
In the distance the paper mill is witless

except for a single beam above us all
meant to warn the pilot flying too low

that death is a phallus of mortar and stone
and he lifts his plane heavenward with the slightest

touch of his hand and is transcendent. At such times,
easing my foot off the pedal I imagine

the suicide under my care at Mayflower Apartments
over a decade ago, when I would rise hourly from my desk

and withdraw the flashlight, flicking it on and off
to see if it still shone before descending

into the underground garage of gorgeous Camaros
and Porches, cold to the touch after midnight and abiding

side by side, which I peered into with my light
leading the way. After so many years

I admit my guilt for sometimes stopping
at the door to merely observe and going no further,

driven back by the chill and odor of gasoline.
I cannot align myself with Cain anymore and say

in response to a curious God, "Am I my brother's keeper?"
I was naïve, believing the imagination placed

me above blame and bitterness borne of living
in a universe indifferent to this, someone I never knew

cramming a towel into the exhaust pipe of his Ferrari
and waiting for death to appear, a drowsiness

making it hard to lift a hand against the killer.
Those who spoke of him later knew that he

was doomed and had tried to soothe him.
I would have told him the truth and excluded

nothing, alluding to the story of a man
who left his wife and child alone one night

in a rage over potatoes cooked too long
only to come home the following dawn to find

them dead, the daughter face down in the bath
while overhead her mother swung from side

to side as though blown by wind as listless
as a summer's breeze, and lifting her

learned he did not want to live with the guilt,
putting a pistol to his head and nearly

squeezing the trigger when he heard a voice
opening into what I can't describe

commanding *Don't* and he indignantly complied.
Would he have accused me of imposing my precious ego

upon the poem, declaring himself alone
with the love of death? But I did not know him.

And so I sat at my desk that night in the lobby
revising, cutting line after line until the sentiment

of endless love had been ground down to a stanza
even I did not believe, while you leaned back and breathed

deeply and were eager for life to be over
and death to begin. That did not happen.

I let the hour pass and the hour after that,
crafting the stanza and noting my supposed vigilance

over the parking lot outside the garage
you stumbled from when your gauge lay on empty.

I did not see you until the three policeman
burst through bearing a folded stretcher,

"There's been an attempted suicide in 322,"
and moved away and were surprisingly cool

at the elevator door, letting the paramedics enter
with a wave of the hand and they ascended together.

I remember and choose to forget the attempt
at suicide that lay open the tender flesh

of your wrists and splashed your bathroom
with a stain your roommate couldn't scrub away

for days, a death that fought fiercely
as Jacob in the grip of a tireless angel

and then relented when you were raised
onto the stretcher and carried quickly away

complaining the paramedics were not gentle,
the front doors opening to an ambulance

frantic with light. I remember and I lied.
Why not corroborate my story by pointing

at the page that signified the hour and my rounds?
But sometimes driving home at night

I see the nightmare again and believe everything
is possible, self-sacrifice and brotherly love and death

with more dignity than a speechless shape on the bed.
I cannot bring you back yet resurrect you

in memory passing the paper mill tonight,
maybe to explain why the imagination

lies dormant until the fear of death comes clear
to the human being, or until the love of one

becomes the love of others so completely
we forget why we were ever enamored of ourselves.

FROM
CONSTANT LONGING

Evening Inventory

I wanted to praise the moral quality
of the black ant, the ministry of the heron,
the dove that built a nest above my door-sill,
the potato for being so blunt, the bread,
the brown field, the bashful blue Columbine,
my careful account of what I had seen that was needed.

 How easily the worn soul comes now to peace
with the appearance of the apostle of a tree.
Its logic is of the dawn
and of the evening. Let me endure
in my grandeur, in my dark poverty, my wild ways.
With all that follows. With all that flows and sways.

 And I am in love again with the light
on stone columns of the cathedral
riding the silence of the mind, with sympathy
for the fist clenched against winter: Larkspur,
thistle, slate and quartz—Yellow Sand Verbena.
Names. And situations. And the strong heart that stays.

 The firmament falls back; the constellations slide.
Sleep comes to the Wild Gourd,
the Globe Lily, the hawk in silhouette.

The ecumenical council of the crows has ceased.
And another spirit that does not speak
sees everything: Primose, Mariposa, Golden Pea.

The Snapping Turtle at Templeton Pond

        My friend once reeled something in
from far off, pulled up from the floor of a pond
when he was a kid, neither swerving from one side
to the other (but clearly alive) nor fighting back,
a great weight that finally showed itself under
the surface as a shape darker than water with glints
of yellow. "It burst up," he said, "its forefeet braced
on concrete, as if it wanted to see what had done this,
then snapped the line." My friend's eyes widened

      but I was lost in the descent,
a ribbon of blood trailing from my jaw
until at last I settled along the bottom.
A cloud of silt rises up, fish flick away
as if of one mind, a wreath of weed waving
from around my neck. Then memory fails me
after an hour of stillness and circumspection
from the depths, and I am left to dwell
on a disturbance of the heart—the knowledge
of what sought me out of all the turtles in the world.

        And then, of course,
everything forgets me—and is forgotten.
I work free the hook, scraped along the flesh
of my palate, it sways off, borne upward by the nylon line.

If you see me
in your sleep and feel the fear of death
because you understand, if you think
me a deity that willingly drew close,
certain at first I came against my will,
picked me up, peered into my eyes,
felt the need to prepare for the inevitable
you got wrong, gazing up like a brutal patriarch
awakened by laughter in the middle of the night,
remember: I am what I am and have
no choice. If you want me to be a god
it should have told me
and I would have dragged you down into the dark.

Laundry in Venice

(for Fran Levine)

Your painting Laundry in Venice came today
and I have to tell you I was shocked

at just how beautiful it was,
so finely done I studied each subtle brush-stroke

before putting it up on the wall of my study. Of course
it brought back memories of you showing me slides

last August outside the laundromat in Vermont,
too modest to accept my praise for your accomplishment.

In your letter you inquire about my writing.
Last December I was there for the death

of a friend and unsuccessfully tried
to write her into a poem that went nowhere.

I wasn't sure what anyone could say of a life
lived so much off to the side, remembering

the photograph I saw of Stephanie at eleven
in the camera's eye with her cheerleading

outfit on and finding it almost impossible to fathom
God would have the audacity to set before

this girl the dying she would endure
for seven years. She seemed so thin,

looking shyly out over the passage of time,
to ever be touched by such pain.

But touched she was. Those of us who loved her
let her go because we had no other choice,

having watched her struggle to stay alive
so many years. Once, when she was in Texas,

she sent me a postcard of the hospital,
M.D. Anderson, which simply said on the back

"Dear Dennis, having a wonderful time,
wish you were here." And I thought if someone

having a bone-marrow transplant could still retain
her lightness there was hope, not only for her, but for us all.

She fought so hard, with fierceness,
through chemotherapy that turned her skeletal,

heroic, an outcast with an outrageous wig
that struggled to conceal what she was going through,

fought against the notion of her mortality
and the conclusion that she would have to come to

that everything she held most dear
would be left behind. I delighted in making her laugh

till she was in tears, in the pleasure she took
in showing me around her garden before she died,

pointing out each flower, calla lilies and chrysanthemums,
the time we danced together at Ed's wedding.

How beautiful she looked in her new swimming suit
the summer her husband and I broiled miserably

in the heat at Lake Nichol. I wished, but for her,
we were sitting before an air-conditioner, drinking cold beer.

Foolish to imagine what wisdom she must be blessed with
certain she will be waiting for me when my time has arrived.

Do you remember our walk to the house we thought
was Robert Frost's? That woman

with her back to us as we came up
haunts me still. From behind she looked exactly

as I imagined Frost—short and squat,
with a shock of silver hair. And I remember

how cordial she was, not getting up
from her chair and strangely letting us walk

around her house: you, me, Tracy,
Andrea, and Jill. Didn't we even go in?

When did we realize this wasn't
Frost's house at all, that she was merely staying here

and that Frost's house was further on?
Was that after we left or did she inform us

of our error while we were there?
And I remember asking you about the life

of the first poet I read and loved so many years ago,
James Wright, when I was in my twenties,

and you told the story about his visit to Fresno,
the glass of vodka filled to the top at breakfast

because Phil made the mistake of saying
"Just say When," the poet as tender in his poetry

as one can get without going mad, and bitter too
because what he cherished in this world was

being defiled, the kind of poet I idealized once
and tried to mimic but that I consider

differently now remembering he was human
and doing what he could to simply survive.

I first read his poetry when I was a roofer
in South Dakota, over twenty years ago,

and I still have what looks like a rash
across my knee, having clumsily allowed

that hellish fluid of hot tar to find its way
through a slit, affixing itself to my skin.

And I remember, too, one weekend took us to a city
where we spent three nights up the street

from the theater whose roof we had to strip,
peeling back that ancient layer in the heat

before preparations for the new roof could begin.
Beyond the trees lay the glittering Missouri,

ultramarine in the distance, and while I resolved
to throw myself in at the end of every day,

after I had taken a shower and had a few beers
it never occurred to me again.

I looked at that river with the same craving
I did those thunderheads that murmured

on the horizon then turned left over the plains,
God's fault, whom I rebuked in silence in my heart.

And it was strange being awakened in the dark
by another man, the fist at the door

followed by "Dennis, get up!" and I would lie
and listen to the fist all down the hallway

then put my feet on the floor. Next to my bed lay
The Branch Will Not Break. And I would pick up

Wright's book and slide it inside my bag
so the man wouldn't think I was crazy, the prospect

of returning on a day humid and blazing, of climbing
that long precarious ladder which would lift

just a little as I stepped out onto the roof
even with the treetops, one I didn't relish in the least.

If the poet knew what I was doing in that room
he would have been appreciative, don't you think?

But what I am leading up to, Fran,
is that my last night there I discovered

coming up the stairs no matter how many books
you've read there is a bewildering flipside

to the good life I had lived, all whining
about an unjust world washed away by awe

when I walked out into the hallway lit
by one ceiling light and heard a voice

neither feminine nor male crying from one
of the rooms off to my left. Were they calling me?

No. They were beseeching nothing in this world,
not God, nor the nearness of loved ones;

not the hope of a life that would eventually get better
from the darkness I knew looked just like mine.

I felt pity for all women and men and was afraid
of opening that door to a figure reaching

out its hand to me and that, without saying anything,
would beg me to stay throughout the night.

Then crying ceased, although I waited long
for it to revive, inching back into the shadows

when one of the other men emerged from his room,
a towel wrapped round his waist. Next morning

I found that door wide open and the bed made,
every trace of their being there swept clean.

It would be twenty-five years before I understood
what inspired that cry and what it meant to me,

carrying Stephanie out to her father's van
the day she died, in her blue and yellow bathrobe.

Every now and then she would lift her hand
in the mirror and groan and I wanted to scream

when the lights turned red on me,
cutting recklessly in and out,

traffic emphasizing what Auden meant
about Icarus falling into the sea,

that life goes on no matter what
and the slightest hint of weakness

can be our destroyer even in a dark red van
veering north with a family perfectly aware

their daughter will not see the sun again,
her cry coming again despite what Stephanie's

mother said when I looked back at her,
that Stephanie didn't feel anything.

But our walk was a memorable one,
in the heat and shade of a gravel path

through the Vermont hillside,
then up the highway with pastures cast in soft light,

one I hope to repeat someday
if there is any justice. It is June,

and what I originally thought was a mockingbird
sings from the upper branches of a hickory

across the street so passionately
you'd think it knew of something that could not

be denied, like your desire to affirm for me
while looking up at laundry

a world beautiful and ordinary and true
with that Italian morning opening wide.

What Is Written Down

Call it love gone wrong or something
just as deceptive and you find yourself fumbling again
in the light of the porch for the key
during that interim at twilight
when the neighborhood's empty
and the woman in pin-curlers stands
at the kitchen window washing dishes
as symbol of the life you could not live.

This is the witness turning back again
to the canticle of blossoms borne across the lawn
on an afternoon when no one comes through
the door to inquire why,
to inquire where,
written down in language in love with itself,
a conversation with the dead
that stops at the threshold of the century,
a monologue of jumbled praise that has
as its brother, solitude, its sister despair.

This is the testimony of the leaves
torn from the hickory in bleak November
revised and clarified
till only the mysterious truth reveals

what's left of a marriage
is not the issue, and never is.

Death is the issue, and what it does
to the chameleon that sees clearly
each petal relenting in the garden
behind a two-story house where someone
still frets over the lateness of the day, the season,
Stephanie preparing dinner in her bathrobe,
shadow among shadows, almost a shape,
shooing a moth through the window
with a hand that never looked so pale and thin.

And out of this revelation appears
a purposeful figure bereft of everything
that's cherished, a specter
come from some other place
to show you the way was not the way,
the path not a path, and all your preparations
a waste until you can explain
to yourself why you believed you even needed the key
now disengaged from its chain
to get you through the entrance no longer there.

Blue Photograph

—Alabama coast, spring 1995

If you were going in search of a single theme
that would redeem you, this driftwood
off the coast would be to your pleasing,
imprisoned within the lull and sway
of the sea, within the vertigo of ferocious water.

In a script like that of an animal's hieroglyphics
in the sand, nothing of what you witnessed
can be translated
where land and sea face each other in enmity.

Alone on the beach, in this blue photograph,
your eighty-two-year-old father stands in an open jacket
with his pants whipped back against his shins,
your mother sitting with a camera that won't flash
then does. When you told him

> this was the photograph you loved above all the others
> he was shocked. Time claws
> at the mind,
> and the three of you ground down by a multitude of

suns reject that archaic craving
erased as it is being realized toward whatever future
is left to unlearn.

Pig Iron

      The City of Dis begins with the smell of pig iron
making you sick. At night,
        when factories shut down and the neon

above the Bangkok Message Parlor flashes on,
        you can see the dead
sorting the living into the damned, the redeemable,

      the sure deals shouting commands,
telling us what we loved wasn't enough. You can see
        the flow of people dressed in sweat pants

under the trees that line the polluted lake
        in one of the suburbs
where a woman watches her Pomeranian shit in the public gardens

      with the supreme indifference of an angel
and death follows a child of eight
        who cuts into the woods alongside the highway

because supper is waiting. In the city of mutilation
      God is ground down
and people touch each other tenderly on a screen,

       the surgeon's hand rests delicately
on the forehead of a stranger and an ambulance weaving through traffic
       misses a yellow Cadillac by inches.

       And when the sun glints in the eyes of those coming in
at the mall on One-hundred-Twenty-fifth Street
       the moon appears, and from the inner brilliance

of a kitchen in one of the high rises still lit by the sun
       after twilight, a voice
in the city of sacrifice, the city of pain,

       begins to complain. And you can do nothing
for the suicide sitting on the edge of a bed at Motel 6
       with all of it coming at him,

in the city of revelry where nothing matters
       and even a candle asks too much, in the city of grief
where the only relief for the pain is the needle's

       slow insertion. A teenager dressed in red leather leans
into the window of a Porsche before getting in,
       and repentance comes with the sun just cresting the steeple

at St. Jude's Hospital where the deity nobody needed
       bends beseechingly,
ready to come back and finding it hard to break free.

>   Then sleep. And in this sleep a creature
> undressing before a mirror
>   allows herself to be touched before turning away.
>
> Taking my way home across the bridge
>   overlooking the city, with my window lowered,
> I looked at shadowy figures along the ditches, the whistle
>
> announcing another shift, smoke stacks trailing their banners
>   indifferently above the misery
> of strikers too bitter to have mercy, holding their palms out to the fire.
>
> I was alone and late in understanding
>   what it takes to go back over everything,
> ransack the past, see if there wasn't something I could
>
>   have done, kind words whispered to the adulteress
> across the pillow, cupping her hands,
>   saying my name so softly it seemed a blessing.
>
> And I can't keep the days from fleeing,
>   scent of bonfires and the traveling
> of blackbirds across the heavens: a river of minutes, hours, seasons.
>
>   Gone is her white nightgown so thin
> I could see her thighs,
>   gone her leg over mine, the light flicked on

after midnight and the face in the mirror
        at the mercy
of a stare too cruel to be refuted by my mind.

Reading Habits

I always look for the small poem first,
the message tucked inside the stanza
stiffening against
any effort to correct what can't be said
in any other fashion.

Like staring at a sketch
by Michelangelo hinting at something grander,
an inconspicuous countenance
discovered gazing up in his Last Judgment
where even pride is abandoned.

Devotional

Let's erect a tomb to someone stupid,
one antiquity can't match
nor the ancient civilizations of India and China.
Make it massive and immovable
against the earthquake's fury;
a monument to the accomplishments of yours truly.

There will be a citadel, like an upraised finger,
meant as a guide for the humorless
traveling by sea, the penitent, the devotee,
with rumors of instantaneous healings,
of demons wrenched from the ear
from gazing at this monstrosity to me.

It will persevere long after the millenniums,
long after the Mediterranean has turned to silt
and death can't be remembered
and time no longer whittles away at the skin,
a stupendous tomb, crafted by hands
too numerous to fathom, impervious, clean.

Let eternal longing possess my corpse completely,
my bones, my fingernails, my raving mane,
decked in emeralds, with all sorts of insignias,

a tomb scented with frankincense and myrrh,
and with a labyrinth that grieves
for the one who sought to save herself in me.

Litany

When Thomas Hardy let himself be dragged

to a local tavern by his companions
(who felt he was not having

    fun),
he looked out a window for hours

at a cemetery while they roared with laughter,
prodding him to join in.

Let this simple blessing remember him.

And when everyone cried out
at Descartes to come forth and be merry with wine,

    women and song,
he packed all he had into a carriage

    and escaped to the country,
      temporarily at peace
in a cottage surrounded by wild chrysanthemums.

And when Franz Kafka read *The Metamorphosis*
    to his friends

they thought the story was hilarious.
And he fled back to his desk
where nothing could appease his hunger.

And when Boris Pasternak got a call
one night from Stalin
who wanted to know

why Pasternak was going out of his way to defend
Osip Mandlestam

he invited Stalin to have a talk

about life and death,
whereupon Stalin abruptly hung up.
And when, dressed up
to look like one of the more famous painters

of the day, one of Henri Rousseau's
close friends
knocked on his door to say he had come

because one great painter ought to pay homage to another,
Rousseau with a smile responded
"I have been waiting for you for a long while."

*

To write the story of love and death

        one long continuous thread
   enters the flesh
                and separates the minstrel
from the rest, the Dean, the Doctor of Internal Medicine,
the Receptionist. I lift my pen.

What it means to be among the living and the dead.

The Leopard

The living have many faces; the dead, one.

When the leopard comes down out of the forest
everyone is awed. It comes down

without a sound through the long grass of the savannah
bypassing the herds of Thompsin's gazelle

in the glow of the moon on a cloudless night
beginning to glide toward lights this side

of the river, a swiftness
startling a bird straight up. We hear the cry

of the hyena again, maniacally happy over the death
of a wildebeest dragged down from behind

as the leopard slows then comes to rest
across the road from a Somali woman and child,

then later drags that child up into the trees
to keep it from being devoured by the lions.

There, where screams can be identified
by the hyena at night, the leopard crouches

at the base of a tree before it leaps
lost in leaves concealing everything.

At dawn the leopard licks its paws
no longer hungry for the heart of a child

disemboweled alongside a limb in early fall
where the eclipse of the moon shocks

even the strongest warrior
and the leopard sees us for who we really are.

The Anaconda

The man with the anaconda around his neck
seems proud, letting it coil and slide

across his outstretched arm and cupping
the throat as gently as a sparrow.

He has arrived
to flaunt his fearless love at noon

to traffic on the highway,
wrapped up in this tough-minded muscle that shares

his days in a cage of glass demanding all,
flickering his tongue, the habitual

tic of a thief alone in the night,
thick and glistening, threading its length

gently up around his shoulders now
and weaving the delicate wedge-head in the air.

The anaconda does not seem to care
that it will be carried out to be admired

on Greensboro Avenue with its master
smirking at those who linger along the highway,

as if he alone possessed
the courage to confront this gliding dream

embracing everything. The anaconda feels
but begins to hunger for something other

than what it feels, flashing
between the master's spreading feet,

projecting its sexual head
like a wild idea, looking behind and around,

like a hand thrown up by a child,
nude, with nothing human on its mind.

And when the master grows tired
of presenting this labyrinth of flesh to the crowd,

folding and unfolding above the ground,
too feverish to receive his several kisses

offered to demonstrate his love,
he unwinds the willing creature with difficulty,

pouring it into the cage beside his bed
with patience won from things done right,

as if the anaconda were the embodiment of knowledge,
or consciousness wedded to consciousness

in a moment of clarity, hidden in stillness:
vainglorious, passionate, precise.

Shadows

    In photographs of the frozen dead
near Stalingrad, there is a gesture,
      the hands and feet outstretched
as if to express what it is like to be impaled
    by a bayonet

    yet remain this side
of death. "Who do you love?
Who do you desire more than anyone else?"

    And on the streets if you look closely
you can see shadows cast by the gutted storefronts
where somebody has stumbled over the corpse
    of a cart-horse

    burned black in the aftermath,
shadows that shrink back,
  vanish,
lengthen over the rubble in the other direction

    till they are swallowed up
and the moon
    clears the only tree for miles around

with this perpetual question: "Who did you die for?
Who will you sacrifice?"

And in the story of Christ
before he capitulates there is this instant
when he regrets everything,
as if he hadn't the heart for this, absolute agony

like the screaming hinge of a door,
stopping everyone in a circle of whirling grit,
including the initiate
who has taken her place beside the high priests
in their ceremonial hats

and the soldiers who are supposed to know
what they are doing. Mary
is helped to her feet,
Christ lifted almost gingerly, wrapped in white linen
with a thin strip around his neck,
enabling anyone
to flick back the head covering in answer
to the question "Who is this?"

Separated, at last,
from those who would let you suffer
another death,
your faith questioned by your lessors,
did you ever imagine the furnaces of Buchenwald

> might come to pass
> walking out with the rain beginning to fall
> all over Galilee, your silence broken
> and the voice of your rough companion calling after?

Original Pleasure

Summer understands what summer loves,
the path to the house around a grove of hackberries
standing with their hands up in the air,
an anecdote about one
flamboyant flower bestowing orange petals
on the asphalt—dew on window sills.

The drunken hum of bees above a blossom
pleases, as does a dark barn,
bats at twilight flashing below the moon,
wind in a blue and wandering way
diminishing around midnight and two women, nude,

nearing the wide lake of their dreams
where they darken with the water
lukewarm in June. A chrysalis
comes first, soldered to the underarm
of a birch, in summer's love of what
is overlooked by eyes like mine, mosquitoes

confessing their secrecies in malicious prayer,
the toad alone below the tulip
smart as a Buddha. Sandra,
I like the way you arrived at a pool
in your poem, moving as summer moves.

To understand what love is
is to be ravished by language, by August
already gone, withdrawn from under the touch
of one who loves too much
each leaf and labors daily to regain
original pleasure—the greenest hue.

(for Sandra McPherson)

In the Light of My Lamp

You are a spider and yet
I count your legs to only seven,
daddy long-leg marching across the blank
page of my typewriter then over
the portable phone, all legs
with a dot for a body like a dilapidated ladder
unfolded—no one would think of Coole
and that missing swan
but the one who looks at you this Sunday,
speechless Muse, Minerva,
suddenly pausing I know not why
for the longest time
beside my elbow in the twilight of my house.

Here. You have nothing
but the enigma of our being
to live with for a minute,
the page you make nothing of
as if sentences were better unsaid,
speech unreceived. What dank
corner have you chosen
to be alone, only to reappear
years later to someone else
when I am long since gone? Golden

in the light of my lamp and reluctant
for reasons I can't imagine
to walk off with great strides,
I'd like to give you this
and know that you existed,
puzzled over, one leg gone,
with grace going up and over and out.

FROM NEEDLEGRASS

For the Dawn

What comes to me now comes slowly
and I am alone
with the death of everyone
I have known, with my daughter
dressed as if for a wedding
in the dark of this first morning,
this first night,
my oldest sister in silence
outside the door that will not open
until time is no longer time
and the heavens fall.

It is the ocean
before the sun, the waste of water
borne through the night,
that lets the beginning
and the end become finally
what I can fathom. The face of a god
crumbles to fine dust.
My love of a woman disperses
like seed through the air.
One star steadies itself.
It goes out. Now I am no one.

And the sound of the waves
is the sound of the shameless
chasing after what never was.
Water to green water. Give me
the heedless world again.
Come toward me, mustard weed.
My own heart stops hurrying.
More than the sun. More than the light.

I wear the ladder of sky,
a bare tree twisting upward
like the still flame
gliding slowly back to me now
lighter,
meadow of lupine, gorge of black rock.

My father finds peace.
My mother weeps in the dawn.
And it is final
and it is beginning
in this place below the dark.

Midnight of the Word

Hawks ride high above the prairie, circling, circling, and as the prelude
to the thunderstorm wind, along with the sudden dark, drives birds
to their nests and brings men running out to their cars to close
the windows. Then quietness, the wind is listening—
   then that brilliant whip of lightning that summons you out

of the house looking there, then there—the second flash caught
out of the corner of your eye. It is high summer. And your uncles
drink Storz beer from their steins, burping and smoking in the den.
"We need this rain," Uncle Harlan offers philosophically,
   and the others nod. Then lightning shakes the world again. Feel

the reverberation stutter up through the foundation of the house,
up through your legs. Peer out the window into the street stunned
by the stillness of maples faintly illuminated, quivering. North
Riverview is dreaming, the whole city in a vast
   communal sleep that suggests you are the only one up in the world,

that for this protracted moment in front of the latticed pane
what you think is significant, the voyeur at ten turning over notions
vaguely ontological. That time might be suspended. That the lamp
left on in a single house implies a crushing loneliness, and within
   this hovering stillness that asks for nothing, nor settles for less,

a disposition of spirit lives. Back through years and everything comes
down to your silhouette at the window in your pajamas, against which
the unshakable feeling of separateness is measured. In the dusk
above the yellow blossoms of the four o'clocks, sphinx moths
   maneuver, a blur of wings drawing nectar, in delicate hesitation.

They fling themselves in a violent arc against the dark and are gone.

* * *

And I come quietly forth reaching my hand, long after my mind
has won this truth for me, readjusting my palm around each flower,
withdrawing it after the moths have rocketed away, lifting it
at their return. One is cupped. Nothing fights harder, a racket
  within both hands, my palms pressed closer to quiet what shows

its head just above the knuckle of the thumb. In summer
a murmuring. Then a hush. Soft wind. A car door shuts. One bird
continues somewhere on the other side of Bonnie Robinson's garden,
continues insistently
  as if to say the end of this day is not acceptable—as if to call those

who know better back—no one persuaded by its singing. The half
moon rides through the sky showcasing a ballet of mosquito hawks
high above the houses—whose lights have all come on—
then lower so one can almost make out,
  in last light, their markings. Whoever looks up knows

this lifting of one's eyes to behold the night and its several stars,
knows this lying on the grass with one's hands entwined
as the occasional meteor burning itself out across the cosmos,
knows this cloud passing before
   the moon directly overhead, as neither far nor near, here

nor elsewhere, spelling out in images what stitches the seasons
together, etching a splay of wrinkles at the edge of a father's eyes,
rots the molar, shudders a wave of gold across the prairie while
enticing a purple wildflower fringed with magenta
   up from a crack in the abandoned parking lot. In secret it searches,

unhurriedly, as if to proclaim: This is just one life, and death
puts out the light in the housefly, the bullsnake skidded over,
twisting—one final irrelevant flick—the caterpillars in their nests
in the cottonwood gone up in flames
   and my father standing back flipping open and closed the silver

lid of his lighter. Lean nearer.

Eden

Not a care in the world
caressing the winged limb of the ash.
Or crouching to chart the path of the black ant.
The iridescent spectacle of wasps
coupling in mid-air above the white impatiens
is touched on by the light—
huge ferns   dogwoods   tulips opening wide
chickadees   bluebirds   wrens
everywhere an assertion of singleness.

But it is the symmetry of Eden
surrounded by a gate that can't be located,
curvature and line—motif and theme—
that haunts me when I have lost my way
in the loud world: configuration of snow geese
up which one dreams. Give me
cattle winding back from the pasture,
patterns of the newly created long-
stemmed wildflowers flashing their deep red,
the smell of rain in high cedars.

Dark stones cloaked in algae
glitter beneath the irritable surface of a stream.
And after a while the principle of analogy

is ruthlessly borne upward into
crystalline eyes, the wind
seems like the night sky coming at you,
one thing another in ways bewitching—how,
watching the Indigo Bunting sip
from the cleft of the rock,
loyalty of water to thirst occurs,
night's oneness closes round.
Then maybe the craving to love what can't
be loved without the experience
of evil—the river that speaks of time
in a timeless region. The cricket underfoot
shakes off its death. The resurrected silkworm

goes humpbacked along the lip
of a leaf. Wounds close. No one suffers.
There is no place for sorrow in the heart.
And yet what passes on wide wings
remains, and what's to come
wakes Adam in his bed of straw,
not knowing what to make of his
first reverie along a river
coursing through columbine and sage,
his eyes looking into eyes for what was there
just yesterday—the realization of age,
wind scented with imminent snow.

Linger underneath the silhouette of a great tree with me.
Consider how meaningless its gesticulations

without the hint of decrepitude conveyed.
It is the symmetry of Eden,
distribution of the various and the same,
order beyond the argument for order
that fevers me, the beautiful made more beautiful
because the metaphor looms, like *low mist creeping*
season upon season upon season.
Night like the mind. Like blinding insight
light strikes the wave, and grief
seeks its equivalent in towering cypresses
bent hard away from Eden. Someone is fashioning a key

for which no lock exists
until a fiercer vision intervenes.
It is the first decision, Eve,
the dread of life inspired by the rhetoric
of a snake stretched out in lassitude
beneath a veil of leaves.

At night the memory that I make
of getting up at dawn to sit
with my asthmatic sister, counting the minutes,
of following the flight of the bee
without being able to calculate
which way—of seeing cattle mate—
of sequence and consequence and arrangement...
I think of that first place again
now close enough to touch—now far away.

April Snow

(to Jane)

I came upon your photograph again and followed
what used to be, a forbidden gesture
to be recorded in the ledgers
of the deities—along with that woman's turning
to look back at a burning tower
and the lyricist that just could not help himself.

The park shuts down in a solitude of snow.
Even those bold flowers,
daylilies all, which set out in November to say
again who they are,
withdraw like bridesmaids into a deeper interior
we can never know.

You were beautiful. The long candles lit
on the mantlepiece, you prepared an altar
for the sacrifice that started
with your stepfather hitting your sister in the mouth
and ended in a fall of snow.
I loved the essential sorrow of your story.

I don't want to write poetry anymore,
that wild performance
of getting dressed to the nines to witness the wedding
of light and dark. This is for those spoken
for—by the flute and the lyre.
They come up breathless. They are turned to salt.

What the Rising of the Dead Shall Mean

1.

The dead will not rise up in their coffins.
They will not die again.

You will never seem them cooking in a circle
nor hear at twilight a ruckus to wake the living.

The dead will not hover the half-lit houses
nor carry the wind along.

They will not bless their fathers
and mothers who are endeared to them.

The dead are indifferent to the dead.
They are indifferent to women in dark dresses.

Though you bow before them
the dead do not move.

Though you decorate their graves
the dead do not move.

The dead will not follow you through your room.

They will not sing to you when you are alone.

The dead do not remember who you are.
They do not dream of coming back to you.

2.

                UNCLE HARLAN THAT NOVEMBER DAY
riding a light through the sky
         somewhere back in a time turned darker for the years.

    And the voice learned from the earth,
intones, from the grit of listening shale:

        Mine is the silence of an oak remembering all down
its trunk to the dry dirt of summer

the first leaf of its making,
        down through the massive root,

      the black marl, the molten lava.

    Mine is a meditation of stone turned to earth,
earth to grit.

            What you have come to is a note,
    the names of the long dead marveling

the moment of creation when the voices tremble together

        into a single utterance
only time can obliterate, cough from another millennium,
cry,

        your uncle's laughter
inhabiting a landscape of blown wheat,
sworn to secrecy by the people who would not have it any other way.

3.

        The labor of my father's hands by which
a world grew up
                            around him
disappears with the simple song moaned out,

        and I am listening to the words that have meaning
for me only if the wind quits,
        the night looms darker, his lips whispering through the past.

        I have seen the dead during that hour of mourning
and that hour of joy,
        incipient illumination eked out of the fingertip, squeezed,

light from first light,
the image arranged within a halo of human feeling.

        In that backward glance,
in memory's splendid misunderstanding
    of time and space,

                                            look in your isolation,
in your first yearning,

        for the Great Bear, find Pegasus, Orion. Find un-
created night, repeated patterns of felicity

    woven by a needle stitching the universe,
the sunflower fringed with black still bearing up under the weight
    of a million years.

                UNCLE HARLAN THAT NOVEMBER DAY
and the cocoon cracked open, starved and fallen into my palm.

      It releases me,
a liberation of sandstone wall, meadowlark, mournful dove,

flagrance of bluestem where the nighthawk nests.
        And my father comes forward
in the needlegrass, head tilted as if curious, and the listening begins:

        Someone is waiting

   beyond the hill   beyond deep shade
        of a great tree where horses drop their dung
   in the long grass, swinging their manes   Run

   because you must   past sunflowers   past Denson's meadow
        through the alder grove   it's closer
   than you think   it's right here

Cattle graze

in the pasture where   in a white dress whirling   a girl
      stands   stands absolutely still

and you must never take your

eyes off   for she is changing   she
    in a circle of light   is singing
softly to herself   and you can almost hear her

    And I can trace that rhythm
where I stand,
    that chant married to the movement of bare feet

    when it is noon,
when it has come to night: cold stars, root of Echinacea in my teeth.

    Everything is water in my hands, he says
for he is alone with the shadow
    of such words, feeling the resurrected blizzard

blow across the weather
of his skull,
a breath that urges everything that's still, everything invisible, vast,

    of no significance, to move through this firmament
of shattered glass,
with names like Cassiopeia on the tongue.

With his slender arms outstretched
he catches the sun
    in slow motion, mouth open to receive the sorrowful own at dusk,

    dung beetle, red-winged blackbird, bunting,
waste of the white-tail grazing in late fall.
  Look, he says, I have come to nothing!

4.

UNCLE HARLAN THAT NOVEMBER DAY

    and the three of us lie down among the scarlet globe mallow,

fringed sage and pasque,
    speaking as though to no one, our spirits intertwined,

   the ants in exodus, the coyote crossing into the valley
      catching our
          scent—lie down
and are united in a single dream of riding the night sky

    that never happened, grave after grave long vanished,
that good meal at twilight,

    that kiss, until we can't tell the three of us apart, are neither

    there nor here, are elsewhere,

singing:
>   *You came into the world   there was a cry*

>   *white silence beyond the hospital window*
>   *flew*
> *it would be summer   in no time*

> *fall   turn as you might*
>   *leaves drifted   smoke gave back its beauty*
> *in great swirls*

> *and the sparrow chased the crow   curved off*
>   *wind-driven   you knew what the dark could do*
> *you could see the future   perfectly*

> *it was the present   a man stood up in a boat and laughed*

>   *it was the past*

    There is a grave for the years of getting up before sunrise
to look for the star
   that flees just east of the Pleiades.

   There is
a coffin within great spaces that are themselves a space, a still point

     moving without seeming to.

   In the beginning what withers is what persists, cryptic signature

of the diamondback,
    fragrance of coneflower. Death no longer death. The dance

        you want comes back: those whirling of arms, those chants.
    Where is it? No matter,
says my father, spinning to dust.

5.

Once,
crossing the Missouri River at dawn

                my father felt the surge of power fail

        and cursed the outboard back into sound
but not before that long interlude of going

        serenely in low tones with the almost
unmoving flow: mirror of my father's cigar

    disfigured—perfectly reformed. I know

            now that moment of talking and gliding
holds us, locked in a sanctuary

        of burning glass,
    to be called back when the odor

            of wet stillness and the memory of childhood

under the morning star
                                 come effortlessly together.

                                  My father gives up
to light in cupped hands his cigar then sits back

            to inquire into a life no longer mine. In time
   that earnest conversation is lot.
                             And whoever I am is lost.

6.

Tell me,
in what hour of your going forth,
               your going back,
of all your unions,
                  in what hour would you take with you

anything less
than this, which couldn't be further from the truth

   and yet is not a lie?

7.

That night when I got on the Ferris wheel illuminated like a halo on its side and rose over the upturned faces lifting into the wind, when I knew the elation of looking down at the teenager

tugging on her lover who followed her into the house of horrors,
when I reached the peak and saw on the highway the stream
of headlights and the evening star, a tractor abandoned
for the night on the construction lot, windows in the Hotel Swan,
one with a silhouette watching the aura all around us—
when I descended, catching once more the odor of the elephants,
level with the attendant who turned and spat, drawing his hand
across his mouth, when I stepped back and entered a heaven
of human voices more intimately than ever before and walked
past the sword-swallower, the fire-eater, the bearded witch,
the bumper cars sparking and sliding, I could believe the meaning
of the world lay open in my arms: when I looked up
and away at that wheel of light turning against the night.

8.

The sunflower faces east
and is at peace,
visited by supplicants with wings.
Flagellation of stem and petal.
Unknown root. It is as if in slow light
approaching the talus of a precipice
the reassurance you sought
was being sought in you,
ululation of prairie grass, thistle.
November's rigid senility of trees.
Palm on frosted glass.
All are vanished when the heart
stops flashing its black gown

and the long body of Uncle Harlan
is lain out, white shirt, striped tie,
pale lips of the merry prankster
pursed to resist analysis.

Uncle Harlan that November day
and dead leaves whisper. Curtains
whip inward. What do you seek
if not yourself in these pacific eyes
upturned at evening? Shades
of green. Oarlocks creaking.
Nightbirds below the quarter moon.

And then you too look up:
it's dawn and no one's here.
Or you are in a crowd of revelers
on a morning when wind
scented with honeysuckle
yields up the memory of an afternoon
of yellow and crimson wildflowers in a meadow
just south of Redfield.
And the mirth of many dancers fills the air.

9.

I have had the dream of the dark tree in the field
that falls away from silver sage into the golden brome
with thirty or fourty pronghorns coming eventually to rest
beyond the lessening shadow of a hill,

there to graze, there to sleep standing up
all night until the first suggestion of new light
nears the blue-laden dawn that is dawn for me.
  And I have inquired in that dream.

Where am I now and what am I to make of this
  that has found its way from so many years to where
  I lie in a landscape foreign to me? There will be
  no answer forthcoming, either from within this
  broken-hearted dream, those casual antelope drifting
  like snow over the plains, or when I wake
  wanting what the mind is already in the process
  of forgetting, a leafless tree around which
everything that ever meant anything to me is seen.

10.

I remember how it was in the darkening twilight.
How the sky took on a luster behind the bluffs
just as the sun went down beyond the river.
One idea—that everything falls away, is lost—
shocked me, although I was just a kid looking at a river
throwing a flat rock off the water. You think
all sorts of things when you're a kid looking at a river.
You keep them until the day arrives when you finally
waken into a world you never thought possible: the horizon's
stained scarlet and the long reach of clouds, the wind
beginning to speak forcefully in the cottonwoods. One idea.
Nothing lasts. Not even the silent river at your feet.

Not that first star directly overhead in a firmament
turning light to dark—turning aquamarine.
And you let that truth come at you. You let it sing.

History

Never to lie down again with my sisters in the middle of August
        in a field, listening for that train that comes
        once a day outside Pierre, South Dakota
Never to turn away from the Great Dane Bones
        eaten thin with cancer, at the veterinarian's,
        the injection beginning to work and the look
        of absolute abandonment on his too-human face
Never to sense the presence of those dark downward-gazing eyes
        and the dispassionate lifting of the head
        as I wrote in the light of the kitchen lamp
        and someone I loved called out
Never to reach up, switch off the light, sit quietly
        thinking of my old mother, her fingers twisted
        and swollen with arthritis—of my father's obsession
        with the lawn, on his back those folds of skin
Never to climb again that long ladder as the sun was coming
        up above the high-rises in windless October,
        stepping out onto the roof slick with frost
        until the sun healed me and I backed down,
        shaken by how close I had come
        to flying backward into the arms of the air
Never to stand in a circle of men saying nothing,
        their fingers black from tightening the bolts
        of a winch engine, their soft eyes lifting

       when one of them speaks of a life that has to get better
Or to enter that white house again beside a white meadow
       with someone near, the light on
       outside the porch, already whirling with insects
Just to sleep, and to sleep deeply, without disturbance
       at the end of a day that waits for me on the other side
       of the world
       with the understanding that there is no life but this.

FROM
FOR MY FATHER FALLING ASLEEP AT SAINT MARY'S HOSPITAL

THE NIGHT THE COMET FINALLY SLIPPED INTO VIEW

over the plains,
incomprehensible time

leading up to this long performance across the sky,
it flashed through the cosmos.

What needed to be uttered
was too far back to be summoned all this distance to the tongue.

"God," said my father.
"Good Lord," said my mother against the cold.

And I turned over in my mind a wild idea, beyond what sanctified this night,
the comet steering inward along the heart then veering off—

having come so far so slowly for so long.
And I reveled in the emptiness left behind.

I SEE NOW, BUT I REALLY CAN'T SAY

what lies at the center of what I celebrate, first frost on the lawn,
and the sudden appearance of a beagle belonging to the retired
                                            bricklayer

clearing branches from his gutter up the street, a wanderer through
my living room, Diogenes incognito, as if this were the only way
                                            to behave

and be happy. I am honored and amazed
this day in late October is given effortlessly and allowed a little
                                            breeze,

a reprieve that darkens, each tree needful, considering what this
                                            means,
then regains its gleam and shames the cynic in me with,

O purity of all earth, how could it be any other way? I cannot speak
                                            of the origin
of all creation, of what, if anything, claims the iridescence of a
                                            mud-dauber,

perplexed by my windowpane, that I trap inside a glass and set
                                            free.
What does not want to be known cannot be named.

DEATH, THAT OLD COMPLAINT

so misunderstood, carrying his inevitable coffin,
might fall silent in the wake of such a simple expression—a sentence

that needs no embellishment—because he too is loved beyond his
                                                                                         fame,
because the half-moon shines on the wave, because the song of sorrow

got it wrong, because you had the decency to include him—one
                                                                                       sentence
said directly whose syntax approximates the lacework of black
                                                                                       branches

against a sky at twilight quickly diminishing. Let it be curves
of silvering needlegrass on a hillside in South Dakota driven by
                                                                                      the breeze,

where the evanescent shadow of a sole cloud stays. And geldings graze
next to a barn outside Woonsocket abandoned to wind and rain and
                                                                        mysterious sleet.

BLACK WIDOW, IN THE PREDAWN

streaked with an arabeseque of paint, hole in winter into which I
                                                                                       gaze,
in your negligee of cobwebs abandoned long ago by the
                                                industrious little

money-lenders that spin in another place. Abyss of the open
                                                                               mouth
in sleep. Monotonous night. And this inquisitive lifting of a veil

light as ether to affirm the culmination of a face we thought we
                                                                                 knew,
unknown. Where did it flee? And where will we look for it from
                                                                           here on in?

A CRICKET KEPT ME UP ALL NIGHT

confined to a crevice in the fireplace—disgruntled desert father
that has figured out at least he can sing, if not eat, consoling himself
with the sound of his own making. It continues its sweet supplication

as I run my hands under the tap after breakfast, splash my face.
In a house on the plains
my mother feels this sunlight on her face waking to the radio

and my father too, folded in sleep. What shame is there in imagining
the canticle of a cricket in a fireplace
that does not know any better, working to change what we need?

Something about the dawn. That's what I wanted.
Something that tips the scales for us—that balances the disgust.

SHADOWS IN FORSYTH CEMETERY I PASS THIS MORNING

to the tune of Bobby McGee, belted out by Janis in '68.
Long unwavering darknesses on Halloween. October cast across
                                                                the ponds.

Those bold headstones, mottled by sunlight.
As well as that gravedigger waist-high in a new one by the highway

laboring with a shovel, flinging the dirt.
And I'm reminded of this in my office when I turn

from a freshman essay on Emily Dickinson's dread of the
                                                                inevitable—
and cannot see to see. For just one moment I do not think
                                                            about the pain,

my father taking his medication, getting into bed with help
                                                            from an aide.
Shadows. And at the stern of that great freighter rocking the
                                                            dead to sleep,

creaking, under inexplicable orders to stay where it is,
this image of gravel being hurled as if by no one, golden,
                                             circumscribing the sky.

Turn out the light. Go to Coltrane
as if he were epithalamium—as if he were elegy.

THE APPLE TREE IN NOVEMBER TWILIGHT CAN SLEEP NOW

her journey over for a season
(she did not seem to be moving, but she was).

With her humming with bees I followed her all the way.
First the girl averting her gaze, ashamed,

then her infatuation in April and the shawl of blossoms,
ceremony of her long silence after three days of rain.

I remember the dignity of her deliberations,
how she shook day after day when the downpour

insinuated perfect beauty was a waste.
How she appeared in profile, transfiguring light and shade.

Then the sudden coming together under cover of night,
which I missed (yet imagine against her wishes),

withdrawal into contemplation, a windless shape—blameless.
The worry. And her giving birth.

And the pride she surely took in holding on—
whisperings untranslatable to the visitor in his leather jacket

who stared up at her. Where have you loved?
What are the words for what you have done so skillfully?

I have learned purpose and endured.

A DOE DRAWS SLOWLY OUT WITH ITS HEAD UP

       then browses clover along a stream
       until the hunter and the hunted stand
       face to face—you know the rest
       of the story: the bolt out of dappled sunlight,
       the crack, a trail of blood zigzagging
       for half a mile, then the pursuit through
       thick undergrowth and the question:
       How in the world did this come to pass?

                        This doesn't count
       for much in the mind's fantastic
       pantomime of paired images bent to their meal
       at a long table, the nightshirt lifted
       over the head—the heart in hiding. Here.
       You can have the story of Abraham
       which has nothing to do with love, the glittering
       blade slitting open the throat for a voice.
       Grip the handle. Pull.
       It is the law. A ruthless god exists.

       I drove all summer through prairie grass
       watching the endless rise and fall
       of blackbirds above the corn, certain the origin of
       and simple answer to my longing lay

like a triangle of sunlight on far stilled water.
Past farmhouses, shelterbelts, bluffs,
I leaned into the wheel and encouraged
the little surgeon of a single thought
to do its work, cutting and stitching.
Then the startled exclamation. Then the metaphor

frayed, knitted together again,
the raveled skein spread on a tablecloth
in absolute blackness, with the only light to see by
a light that issued from the mind's
amusement at how everything was the same,
a sweep of cottonwoods
beside a creek bed north of Hayes,
the dragon no different from a wildflower.
The face a map, fingers a catacomb of scars.

LOOK, I DON'T SAY TO MY FATHER

there are stars in a cloudless sky, the moon
at its crescent; there is the drifting night itself,

and the yellow crocuses
under the sycamore in beginning spring.

Look, I don't say, pointing at the dawn
driven by the sun that's yet

to crest the trees, there
is the initiation of another day,

the star of Lucifer, the fading moon,
streaks that waken the wren.

See, taking his hand,
these are the astonishingly long fingers

that danced on the keys
of the saxophone and made it sing,

the bones and ligaments
that strained, the heart that took it all in.

And this my love for you coming out like wind
into the clearing, that cannot help me, rippling the
long grass

at twilight where the first time we observe
the world together without fear.

COME SAID THE NIGHT, AND I WILL FOLD MY WINGS AROUND YOU

come of the darkness and listen to my song.
Away from the river that flows nowhere.
Away from the darkness with me now.

Come said the silence, I will shelter you,
out of your sanctuary of blue and yellow flowers.
Come to the wind and rain and sleet.
Touch this hand outstretched to you now.

Come of the clearness. Understand my sorrow.
Come of the mystery and welcome me in the dawn.
Come of the world. I will be yours
along with that sun, with that moon—and those many stars.

IN THE SILENCE THE YOUNG INDIAN ORDERLY DANAUGHT

shaves you, changes your blood-stained sheets. A blond towel
is tucked up under your chin to support your jaw. This if for your wife
who will sit with you by the crimson lampshade—one hand over the other.
In her frayed cardigan sweater, in her gray corduroy pants, she kisses

you on the brow when she comes in, then stands awhile
over your bedrail looking into your far eyes that no longer recognize,
no longer want anything to do with this brown world.
Death takes our breath away; endless. Without cause.

Incredible the way the dead demonstrate how powerful they are,
their future contained with an expressionless brow,
superior even to the wildest sorrow. To laying on of hands, to libations.
Forget them. Forget this moment in desperate November, one person

speaking to another. What brought the two of you to this moment
is what counts. Carry a candle to the cold balcony and watch the
                                                                         sputtering
flame go out, into this windlessness that includes the evening star.

THERE IS A COLD GOD

who longs for deserts too and turns away from no one,
where the soul, no longer certain of anything,
simply listens to the emptiness of wind and sand—
where the sky at night
never loses its blue and the breath of night-blooming cactus

perfumes the air. I would like to go there with faith in myself,
reading under the leaves of palms occupied by cockatoos,
a place where no one dares intrude
even when I dream of other humans.
Who knows what truth might ruin me as I kneel at still pools

lifting my eyes to every evening sky? At night, when I am frightened
and feel the need for further reassurance,
I would listen to wind unimpeded by anything resembling trees
or dwellings: a howl hurdling over the dunes, a hush—
a heaven of constellations.
How beautiful this search for sanctity now seems to me.

St. Jerome in penitence tells the story
at the mouth of a cave when he looks up and away and is purified
by what is lovely. Where is the source of his forgiving grace?

Andromeda right above my head tonight, the Seven Sisters,
I remember again that frantic hour at the hospital in Aberdeen

that has no bearing on what is,
what was. On what is sure to come. My blessing was the touch.
Small wonder it took me a lifetime to figure that one out.

I HAVE ALWAYS WANTED TO BEGIN

with giving the river the first and last word, lay down the law,
walk out of my body, the wind, meticulous, searching the vermillion

of a far meadow north of Mobridge for something hidden. To give up
this goddamn shadow that answers to no one, find my father beyond

his trying, wind whipping his hat off as he pisses into a ditch.
I would lift his bare foot again with both hands, remember how little
                                                                                   he cared

for the elegance of a western sky wreathing yellow into red
(it could break the heart of a horse)—and cup his ankle. But the ordinary

eyes of the returning close. The dead, dirt poor, just stop receiving.
During the apocalypse the river continues carrying its driftwood the sea.

IN FALL I HEAR THE CRY

from the stadium surrounded by an aura of blue light
just as the boy breaks free of the final tackler
and the man who is his father rises,
quieter than everyone else, in his green windbreaker,
his rolled-up program raised to shield his eyes.

In fall the turned-over field yields to the bark
of a golden retriever, on his haunches
at that threshold that stops with the dark.
He wants to be called, swept into the kitchen,
told to go lie down. He looks over his shoulder.
Goes on barking half-heartedly when no one responds.

Then it is November. The retiree three houses down
rakes leaves toward his bonfire in the dark of Monday night,
at times, when he nears the blaze, a specter—
laboring with something he cannot do without.
In winter my mother spins around
in her threadbare chair and watches a commercial airliner

drift through the clouds. The sorrow she thought she had
figured out gives in to the sorrow that lifts,
in an updraft, the oldest tree in the yard.
In winter the transience of life—

the letting go of all that loved what it was.
What happened to that serious pact with summer

to love the world no matter what the price,
love the questions, touch and be touched—
to the nightly prayer for the voice that is like no other?
What happened to the vow not to drink alone,
and what was going through your mind
when you coaxed a white moth up into a paper cup

one night when you were drunk? To let things flow by,
forget death, focus on fellowship and suppress
your hatred of the cat next door that stalked
and crouched, stalked and crouched,
hunting the cardinal an hour before dusk
before withdrawing to contemplate its loss?

Now wind. Now rain. Now sleet in the Japanese maple
thrashing about. And you with your new resolve
to get up, change what you've become, swallow your pride.
Impossible. Let it be said you had pity on a moth
who bore no other gift to give
to the thoughtless creature of a summer night.

FOR THE COMING OF WINTER UNDER THE HUNTER

"What are you doing down there?"
my mother asked, and from the depths
   of the basement my father answered, "Working!"
   And while she never seemed quite satisfied
   with this, she'd go about her business
   clearing the table of its wreckage,
plates and silverware, while he watched *Rawhide*.

   Drifting to sleep, my mother gone to bed,
I'd listen to him climb the stairs,
   to the click of one light after the other
   and the clatter of coins on his dresser. "What
   were you doing down there?" my mother asked,
   gently now, and he said "Working"
in a voice so melancholy it filled me with fear.

   Many Christmases have vanished
without any revelation of my father's intent
   as he bent to whatever was at hand,
      no extraordinary machine of ropes and pulleys
   grotesque on the dining-room floor. Tonight
      I remember my ex-wife
above the chorus of childen's screams in 1989,

"What are you doing down there?"
and look up suddenly
   from my sanctuary of a story
      my father would have had trouble understanding,
   waiting for him to say
      after a pause timed perfectly, "Working"—
working on a past I only imagined might be redeemed.

SING TO ME. I DON'T HAVE THE STRENGTH

to do anything but sit here and listen. Lay your bald head on my lap
if you wish. This is your death and I don't want to insist
if you can't handle this. Nevertheless a little jingle
would be pleasing: mumbled, hummed, a note or two or three.

When you are finished and the sleep we need (flickering with
                                                  lightning perhaps)
slides like a girl on ice up to the steps of the little red schoolhouse
                                                  outside Woonsocket,
what you hummed and what I thought you hummed will come
                                                  together.

Nothing prepared me for you.

FROM
WITHIN THE SHADOW OF
A MAN

Short Story

This was after Vietnam, when the soldiers that came home
to expletives screamed at them from airport lobbies often dropped out,

grew their hair long, did mescaline and got into fist fights with hippies
who ultimately didn't understand a thing because, after all,

had they ever seen the corpse of a Vietnamese baby staring up at them?
I was working as night watchman at an apartment complex

when one night this curious girl comes up to me at the desk
and begins to flirt, a thin blonde with a milky complexion and a
                                                                frivolous air

who was seeing one of those former soldiers and was having trouble
dealing with his temper. Although he hit her she kept

going back to him, she said, because he had been crippled
by the war and she really believed that she was in love with him.

After that I'd wait for her to show up in the lobby late at night
so we could talk about her problems, which just got worse,

one week a blackened eye, the next her working up the courage
to leave him because he had dragged her out of a bar by her hair.

I'd never met anyone who couldn't be helped, and I thought
if there was just something I could do to protect her. It has been

thirty years. I was naïve to think you could intervene between two
people who are sick and who have come to love their sickness—

the only thing they have that makes any sense. I went as far as to tell her
I loved her one night in the parking lot, making rounds while she

tagged along, delighted to have a sympathetic ear willing to listen
to all he dished out, and she told me she thought I was sweet

and hugged me then went back to her boyfriend who broke the thumb
on her right hand because he thought she had been cheating on him—

this guy I saw only once, with a long beard and long hair, rushing
ahead of her on their way to the elevator with a look that said

I hate everything. I quit not long after that and never saw her again,
but the world that was beginning to draw near me seemed

not nearly as benevolent as it had, and if I ever looked away
would slaughter me then go on whistling its way out the door

in search of its next victim, the one who wanted to be the savior
of if not this man, then that one, and who was certain

love was the cure for everything.

CREED

How garish the cherry tree this April was outside my house,
how weighted down, so full of pink blossoms
and belief, the sun at morning crowning first
those highest up with such deliberation along her brow

you'd think she had been dreaming. And what did she believe in?
If it wasn't in the Eastern blue bird that lived in her for an instant
before turning into a shadow showing the history
of misery eating a piece of bread washed down with sweet water

then surely it was in the passage of time that went on stepping
over the dead in the bombed-out streets leading past the chancellery
into the twenty-first century, without once looking back
because it was so firmly focused on the future. For three

whole weeks and into May she held onto each and every blossom
then one especially gusty morning released pink petals that drifted
in through the window I had left open
covering the floor. And when she took the vague shape

of a trivial whisper passed form the lips of children
and later became the three high notes of the sparrow that sang
while it flew, I had a change of heart concerning the fate
of a world in which a girl has to watch her father being shot

in the back of the head before she is sworn to secrecy,
even if that secrecy does not mean a thing
in the grand scheme, which none of us believes in,
except this old Yoshino cherry tree slow-turning in the breeze

which lifts, then lets her go, half in shadow,
in sunlight fluttering,
as silent now as someone who has stopped talking
and begins to listen, as if for the first time he were being revealed.

Mandelstam

Come to the bough bent down by the vicious wind in the cedar,
the yellowing leaves my brothers, the still green leaves my brothers.

You have heard of the seven emaciated men, blind-folded,
carted off, driven from their homes in a bitter winter.

What about the insidious history of sunlight changing in the maple.
The history of stillness. Of the one inscrutable finch.

They are coming. You can hear the thundering of hooves. The laceration
of braches—the brutal shouts. The upturned eye of the stallion

is my eye, streaming in its socket. My black flanks gleam in the sun.
You know what it is to be ridden and savagely kicked,

the acidic taste of the bit in my frothing mouth. Quick.
Although you desire the singing of the cardinal in spring

they are coming. Although you crave
the repartee of the wren, they will drag you out into the street.

To a Fly Along the Nose of the Generalissimo

You have flown sullenly up from the corpse of a frog in the dust
to instruct the flowing assemblage of mourners
and celebrants and thieves on the threshold
of compelling sorrow, habitually rubbing your fore-legs
and gesturing just above the thaw
of mucous pooling at the base of the impudent snout.

You have drawn the constituents of death inside and nudged
them up into the nostril,
have entered that labyrinth yourself, as a show of support,
and glimpsed that raving Old Testament prophet spouting off
from the epiglottis. One searchlight
sweeps back and forth across the firmament. It is dusk.

And the racket of screeching rigs and bulldozers and human moans
echoes then hollows out along the intricate reticulations
of the craw. What soft counsel
you keep with the interlocutor of spittle—snapping his leather belt.
For it is no good giving everything you have to the clot

on the bloated tongue, to the groove of the mouth sprung open
where ants like pickpockets
fulfill their desperate destinies and the maggot inspects the ridges

of the jaw. You have to be still. At times you even
have to be motionless. To hold
something back is the only way to survive. Where now

is the voice that fluttered in the breeze of Granada in 1936?
Where is Federico Garcia Lorca after being mocked then shot
in the chest? Where the Andalusian plain and the row of cypresses
along the road Antonio Machado suffered over from his room in Soria?
Where is the scent of burning straw in autumn fields that sparked
the rose into composing one more song?

Alone with the 23rd Psalm

I notice the disturbing blood splat looking up
something in the Gospel of John about Christ's mother

but can't figure out at first where it has issued from, then lift
my forefinger to my upper lip and witness the archipelago it has

etched there; and remember I nicked myself with scissors
after breakfast, clipping my mustache. So I will go on living

although it is pure reverie after that. For just such
an unsettling effect John Keats had, coughing

into his handkerchief, Kafka, the flavor of metal souring his palate,
frantic in Prague, in Vienna, saying on his deathbed, "Place your hand

on my forehead, Dora, to give me courage." The valley
of the shadow of death has no freshets, no sycamores quivering

in the wind. I think of it as strip-mined, with huge rigs, derricks,
slithers of chalk-white smoke lifting from the red brick chimneys,

silent except for the occasional bulldozer backing out,
and corpses carried away to the crematoria in carts pulled

by slow plough horses with their heads down, lashed
when they stop instinctively before the man that stands

aside as if to take in all of his accomplishments. My close friend,
asked if his prayers might go unanswered, his wife of ten years

hopeful after her bone marrow transplant at M.D. Anderson, hesitated
with his hand on the doorknob to his Volvo and said, "Then God

can go fuck himself!" And there was terror at the thought
of that defection, and later that her death would send him scrambling

in all directions for a god to hold onto
even if that god no longer wanted his only prayer.

The Noses of Old Men

The old man who bore such a resemblance to Samuel Beckett
came every Sunday afternoon to the Malaysian restaurant
to order his shrimp and lobster sauce. Facing the front window
beyond which a magnificent Japanese maple struck a pose,
its leaves flushed with crimson,
he would devour the same entrée Sunday after Sunday so that finally
the unspeaking waitress would have it waiting for him. His nose
in profile, when he would turn, was aquiline, and for a moment
I could visualize the master in the months leading to his death,
the silence without echoing the silence within. What is it
about old men eating alone that drives me to distraction?
Something no doubt due to myself
grown gray, appalled to consider I will end up like this,
a hunched curmudgeon, in loose slacks, flatulent in my favorite booth,
eyeing the breasts of the waitress indifferent to my penchant
for curry chicken and fried rice sautéed in sesame oil.

*

I stumbled across the poet George Starbuck once so many years
ago in Tuscaloosa at the McDonald's on Lurleen Boulevard
sitting politely apart, unassuming in his bland jacket,
apparently in high spirits for he had his yellow notepad and his books
set out, his coffee and his Big Mac. I would find out later he
didn't have long to live. To interrupt such a gentleman as this
takes courage. Or audacity. Neither of which I have.

So I watched assiduously from a distance as he pulled on his nose
then went back to reading and chewing
absentmindedly. There, I said to myself, is the man
who slept with Anne Sexton and sat through Lowell's classes
with mad Sylvia Plath. And while the customers carried their trays
back and forth before him, I couldn't get over that.
                *

My obsession with hands—
those of the molester, murderer, priest, supposed penitent—
gave way after that to the noses of old men. Misshapen,
pocked, pugilistic, squashed, I'll find myself zeroing in
exclusively on them and forget what is being said,
on flared nostrils that actually terrify because they appear
so cadaverous. Did you know Beethoven would stand
behind his apprentices and watch the notes they struck on the piano?
If they skipped a key he would pinch them and actually
bent down once and bit one out of resentment, on the shoulder,
that square nose of his, like a lion's, detecting I am certain
the cheap red vinegar splashed on as an afterthought to gratify
the great composer known for his temper. According to Berryman's
"Beethoven Triumphant," after he left the parlor where he had
been a guest the armchair Beethoven sat in had to be tossed out—
he was so filthy.
                *

Fear. That's it. I am afraid of the noses of old men,
nevertheless approach them slowly without being revealed as the voyeur
who analyzes their contours, color, concocts a history, forcing
myself at times to peer up into the hinterlands of those caverns
strung with cobwebs, in which Plato stokes the fire and prepares

his lesson on illusion for future generations. Goya, I've heard,
in old age, was defiant, deaf, but he essentially said
he would outlive all the bastards he blamed for ignoring him,
adamant in all respects, except for his squat unassertive snout
that seemed to forewarn that his stand against the rocks
and scissors of the world would culminate in misery. I wish
I had the chutzpa to go to a retirement home right now
and pay for the privilege of gazing at old noses, perhaps
to gently pinch and prod, sniff, comparing what I see to others,
as well as at photographs of those noses when they were adolescent—
without self-consciousness, inquiring of this, of that,
if the nose was ever broken and, if so, how, of damaged cartilage,
of deviated septums, apnea.
*

I believe I am required in this life
both to come to terms with and to study my uncertainties
                                            and yearnings,
but as I speak I realize the unlikelihood that I will ever be
satisfied with just the right understanding concerning the noses
                                            of old men,
which is to say my understanding of self, in relationship to
those closest to me. And what if the subject of my study
                                            should become
enraged as Cezanne became enraged when he was interrupted
at supper by one of his enthusiasts, shoving him up against a
                                            restaurant wall
in the wake of a great compliment with the announcement "I
will not be made sport of!"? No, I could never handle being thrust
up against a wall and shouted at after looking closely at a nose.

*

Cezanne, according to one of his near neighbors, apparently departed
early every morning from his hovel in Aix-en-Provence to paint the
changing
light in the field, while looking, as is told, "over his shoulder as if
in fear
of being pursued." Such behavior is touching, as is the wrath
of Ludwig von Beethoven at being denied his veal or that he was
imprisoned
briefly because he seemed a tramp—until his identity was revealed.
Might I eventually be transformed through some metaphysical
mumbo jumbo connected to this obsession into something
similar to what happened to the government official in Nikolai
Gogol's
story "The Nose," thereafter to walk through the world with a
horrendous sensitivity to odors? Might I in my own mind alone
come suddenly to see myself as a grotesque
nose with no other purpose than to breathe, sneeze, itch,
and twitch? Beckett berated the performance of one of the actresses
during rehearsal and she fled the theatre, weeping; he ran
after and pleaded with that actress to forgive him, thus adding
another dimension to my appreciation of this same man who,
when pestered
to yield up the structure of his plays, in the end relented, saying
when he was in hospital there was a man with throat cancer
who screamed incessantly in the silence. *That* was the form of his
dramas.

*

How could I not remember that particular anecdote
observing the old man in profile at the Malaysian restaurant
and not want, for just a moment, to approach him as I had wanted
to approach the quizzical George Starbuck? *Bon mot!* My own nose,
never examined out of dread, I would in childhood push
back now and then with my thumb in front of the bathroom
                                            mirror to scare
myself, demonic—as if I were a snuffling incubus. And once
I even permitted a house fly to walk the promontory there,
crossing my blue eyes while it washed its hands of all
the guilt we feel for having been the children of our
recalcitrant parents in vanished Eden. I draw closer
to the octogenarian pushing his grocery cart up the aisle
and scrutinize from the side the architecture of heaven and hell,
Alpha and Omega, inscrutable proboscis of the elderly god,
leaning over as if to get a glimpse of that great abyss
from which we issue, into which we disappear.

Barnum & Bailey

The man on the trapeze had fallen and I was alone
in the hospital lobby looking around when I saw the clown.
"Where do I go?" he asked nobody,
in polka dots and red tennis shoes outside in the hall.
Upset with the security guard for laughing,
he didn't seem to know where he was at all.

And I don't recall if I felt pity when he allowed himself to be
                                                                            drawn
suddenly into the arms
of one of the other performers coming through the door.

I took the long way home
and vowed to speak for the sword swallower, those midgets joined
at the hip, that clown
who wept when the doctor on call said the man on the flying
                                                                            trapeze "died
moments ago." Of what happens when death steps back
to study the world for us among so many others.

Another Dawn

The undertaker turns in at Vogler's Funeral Home and leaves
his Lexus running long enough to finish his cigarette,
muttering to himself behind frosted windows. One more drag.

Somewhere off on the Ngorongoro Basin

a gazelle being followed by three lionesses stares the other way,
and Isaac Babel is led from his interrogators in Lubyanka
with *But they didn't let me finish!* as if the future of speech

hung in the balance and history were nothing more

than the justification for having disagreed.
And I'm on my knees transfixed by minnows in a still pool
staring past my face. Whose image is this rippling into oblivion

than coalescing again, with thoughts of minnows there

until a pebble enters the forehead and I am at my desk
dreaming an undertaker in Winston-Salem toiling over a corpse?
I move nearer. It is me those hands flutter over,

bright blue with the bliss of another dawn breaking wide

and clear across the plains. It is Aeschylus. Swedenborg.
It is Clayton Boyle just up the street on Adams Avenue in 1958
who touched the smooth white ass of my sister Linda when I was nine

as if it were the most marvelous ass in the world.

Wrightsville Beach at Night

Quarter moon. Two stars. Wading out with the living room
lights behind me—still silhouettes of three along the beach. One
                                                 flicks a line

out into the sea, waiting with arms outstretched
for god knows what.
Night blows wildly. No gulls. No misery of need. The swells

loom gentle after awhile,
lifting me briefly than letting me down—cradle where I in a
                                               lullaby of breezes
once drifted off to sleep.

Look,
you can do one of two things if you are me and one of them has
                                                    to do
with what is beautiful. This is one life

beneath the sky drifting with Castor & Pollux along
with the dusk and the sea. Death
lets go. Death relents. What loves you sees you leave
and goes on living.

Within the Shadow of a Man

The female cardinal came once daily
to the kitchen window
when I was washing dishes,
twisting its neck peering in
from the forked branch of the leaning sumac
as if it were interested not only in *why*
here? but in what in the world
I did. At twilight I looked forward
to the storms, deliciously belligerent,
along with the winds that preceded them,
the way the silver maple swelled and lifted
in light left on above the carport.
Birds flew closer to the ground then
and quicker. And I began
to speak as if someone other than I
were there, listening to Schumann's
"Symphony No. 1 in B flat major"
after reading how Schumann once hurled himself
into the Rhine out of despair. One noon
a doe appeared in the back yard, foraging,
its head raised every few seconds.
And autumn hurried along its beauty,
finally giving in to the bitterness
associated with winter, which I

found curiously reassuring.
It would be nice to have a girl
call me in from sitting in my green lawn chair,
wrapped in my goose down quilt,
after an hour of watching turkey buzzards
circling above the clearing,
saying my name in much the same way
my mother and my sisters once did.
The fellowship of women and men.
Who needed it? I had my Chow
and the black and white cat perched
courteously before my door in a rainstorm,
as if it had appeared out of nowhere
from a village in Tibet. Getting up
for a drink of water after 2 a.m.
I saw it purring, so I named it Govinda,
a name it drew to immediately
after that. And more than once it occurred
to me just how miniscule I was. And my purpose,
what was my purpose? That Carolina
cardinal insisted this was not my business
although I still read Pascal in fear,
granting myself the fear of women or men
bereft of certainty on a landscape
dusted with snow
the morning I woke to the first day of the year.

Living Alone

I see it almost every evening in the fall
with the light on in an upstairs room.
And once a woman flashed across the pane
coming home—then flashed again—a dance
in early October to music either classical
or jazz. Later I let her whirl
inside my mind, voice of Placido Domingo
on the stereo, a blur of multi-colored scarves
preventing identification of the soul
that sang above the words,
casting a crooked shadow on the wall.

In summer when those stupendous trees take up
their gowns, that house is lost to the driver
on the highway. No winding path
visible beneath the radiance of the porch.
No blossoming white ivy along the walkway.
But sometimes the light itself
can be seen, if the wind is blowing hard,
and I note the terrible loneliness
of the place—and I want to know
what mystery lives within this far enclosure.
Slow my car, lowering the window.

Suppose I was the father of a four-year-old
and found myself not wanting to go home.
Suppose my fingers ached from twisting
a knife along a precipice of bone at Hormel Packing,
meat slung onto a belt making its slow way
toward somebody's fork in Oklahoma.
Suppose my heart was golden
and suddenly I wanted so much more,
pulled in shutting off my lights
before a bend in the road and thought No!
at the last moment. I call this hope

against all odds for a life that falters then goes on,
elusive as the ghost that haunts the embezzler's
tiny mind as he smokes in the darkened
living room in front of the huge aquarium bought
for his daughter. I call this meat flung up
in the face of the foreman. One light. It looks
so peaceful there. The scent of tea. Music.
Human joy. And in a moment of small turmoil
a man is driving at night trying to find a road
that should be there—but isn't.

FROM
THE LUNATIC IN THE TREES

Solitary Cooking

The barred owl that swept before the Lunatic on the gravel path,
settling with such precision on a branch
before thrillingly descending into the ravine this evening,
turned its wide cat-like head and let go a snow white
drip of excrement. Later he heard it hoot *Who cooks for you*
out in the dogwoods, listening while leaning over his gas grill

cooking cheeseburgers, for it to repeat itself, as if it perhaps needed
to make itself clearer. Then he heard again *Who cooks for you*
—sorrowful as any sibyl over the love for one she knows
she could never woo. Barred owl, if you only knew,
you who remain concealed within that stand of timber, alone,
content to be alone, hour after hour outside the study window

where nothing but the night keeps us from being revealed,
if you knew that the Lunatic looks for you,
what you have to sing coming from first far, then near,
that little malicious inquiry *Who cooks for you   Who cooks for you*
that has everything to do with living alone
as if you yourself were just sitting down to dinner.

The Lunatic Lies Down Under the Moon

He's got a little moon up there
that seems as if it could just topple out of the sky
if someone touched the gossamer
that holds it up. Who's staring up at this same
fingernail of light like him tonight,
this innocent half-smile?
—a daughter almost finished with her homework,
her math book fallen aside?

Gerard Manley Hopkins warned of a moon like this in June of 1876
after he had endured the terrible sight
from his monastery room in Stoney Hurst
of his beloved ash tree
chopped down. Who came up with *moon*, with *sickle*, with *harvest*,
with *full* and *crescent*? The Lunatic would like to know.
Meanwhile, he stares and stares
up at this fanged light that wanders over every one of us.

Eating Emerson

An inconsolable sparrow out there in the dark.
Then quiet.

The Lunatic thinks about who this might be
and settles on the ghost of Ralph Waldo Emerson
in mourning. He is mourning
the desecration of his *Selected Essays & Poems*

left out on the ottoman, that the dog snatched up, shredded,
whole passages of breathtaking insight—
like "the mind builds a house and then the house shuts
it out"—strewn over the linoleum. But you can't fault a dog
for devouring Emerson. No. You cannot fault a dog.

Buddie stares up, flop-eared, the last fragile page
of "The Transcendentalist" stuck in his jaw. He cocks
his head, the way dogs do
when they are in doubt. He too has heard that song.

Ralph Waldo Emerson, we are sorry—if that is you.
Whoever you are, come down, come down
and we will make this actual house
your home.

(for Lucia Perillo)

How It Happens

There were the wild turkeys crossing the open field,
a dozen of them, preposterous in how they walked, like scholars,

so heartbreakingly familial he had to fight back tears.
Then the smattering of Eastern bluebirds

giving their orange and blue to the sycamores
beside the chain-link fence. The barred owl hooted

somewhere near in the ordinary dawn, seven times,
then stood still on the horizontal branch of the white pine

from morning until supper, turning its slow head.
"Wisdom," said William Blake,

"is sold in the desolate marketplace
where none come round."

The Lunatic thought he understood
the relationship between wisdom and suffering,

suffering and love. He hadn't.
But that barred owl bothered him enough

to make him think,
those wild turkeys enough to make him almost weep.

And those bluebirds, ah
those bluebirds bore him away on a dream.

The Lunatic and the Sun

The sun has been, for about a week,
companion to the grass that brightens, dims, brightens,
according to the caprice of the clouds,
off to the side of that conspiratorial family of Porcini mushrooms
in their white nineteenth-century fedoras beside the wooden fence
that separates the Lunatic from others.

The sun, it is such a fine manifestation—
what his thirteen-year-old dog keeps discovering
pushing up to flop down
after a gradual shadow has covered it completely.
The Lunatic touches the warmth of his dog's black coat
when it ambles in,

and remembers his intention to set aside one whole day
for the consecration of sunlight
that touches just as lovingly the evening primrose
as it does the warehouse's red brick wall on Seventh Street
—to consecrate, that is,
by pulling up his lawn chair while balancing a glass of gin

and watching the fleeing irradiating shimmer on the hemlock,
then later that congregation of hovering golden-winged gnats

which shifts as sunlight shifts,
ecstatic for perhaps an hour—
as if floating under the surface of a stream.
This is the gift, this is the promise of summer,

poles of light pouring through the silver maple,
the fringed Fosteriana tulip closing, as though over an empire,
at evening. And the Lunatic in the thick of it
with just a subtle tongue of sunlight
licking his left cheek
as another night comes on, as the horizon blazes.

The Lunatic at Prayer

The propaganda of the bull frogs was enough,
the camaraderie of the wind in the cottonwood trees.
Speech was enough—the long lament of the geese.
Still, the Lunatic returns in memory
under Cassiopeia to those quivering wind-swept dunes
that shadowed the nude blue estuary,
the cormorant drifting north
over Gulf Shores where he stood once alone
under a sky as aquamarine as the inside of a sea shell.

Now the prayer that the prairie moonlight whispers incessantly.
Now the touch of the palm on the surrendering forehead,
now the feast for the poor in spirit, the poor at heart,
the harvest moon over Wessington—over lower Brule—
and that delicate western meadowlark twittering in its sleep.
And the Lunatic mumbles something unintelligible
to the night wind scented with sage,
while a melancholy Holstein
beside a salt lick in the west pasture, bereft, bereft,
throws back her head and bellows.

The Lunatic Considers the Universe

The Lunatic cannot understand why
we don't just fly along with everything else
off the face of the earth the way an ant, say,
is shaken loose from the hand.
Gravity, that mystery, keeps him here.

It is pleasure to walk beneath the whispering dogwoods.
It is pleasure to pause before the foraging bee.
Fat chance we'd be flung far and wide.
Gravity, that mystery, holding us down.

Earth circles, spins—the solar system too—
and still a cosmic serenity sweeps over the Lunatic
watching light, shadow, moon.
Enter the cathedral at night—gravity, more than God, his friend.

To turn inward; that's another matter.
It comes in a rush
like the tearing of silk, the self
peeled back.

ANT

A logarithm, a moving freckle,
a fierce divinity,
goes in search of the grail
throughout the day
and finds this fleck of Wonder Bread on the table,
lifts it like a little Hercules,

carries it away.
It is part of a delegation,
silent in several languages,
spreading out
like the magisterial reflections of the sea.
It has set out from its priory

knowing exactly what will be,
Ezekial, Tiresias,
traveling the broad escarpment
of the porch, under the closed door,
along the wall
and up the pedestal of drawers

leading to this crumb that means so much,
left on the table. Over the course
of time, eternity, an ant

argues in favor of continuance,
creeps, flees, fearful that what it wants
belongs to another.

And takes it anyway.

On the Streets of Honolulu

An elephant has broken loose
and doesn't know where to go
on the streets of Honolulu,
swinging its liquid length of trunk,

after goring the one
that groomed and trained it
to entertain the crowd
paying to see the elephant do something unusual,

like lifting its massive hoof
over the head
of the woman in leotards heroically waving,
to dance and sway,

fettered to a post
along with obedient others nodding and shuffling.
For why else would it react as it has
and lumber up the avenues

past station-wagons and vans, chasing people
and even knocking one down
who has stumbled
and stares up at something

as unforgiving as an elephant at mid-day?
Oh the rage
and uncontrollable ecstasy of discovering
what it means

to suddenly become
in the famous weather
of Honolulu what everyone suspected,
a brute with huge bags

under its eyes and a bone to pick with the world,
thrusting the chain-link fence aside
that stands in its way,
an elephant swaggering and filling up the air

with its wrath
as it goes it knows not where,
perplexed in its red tasseled cap.
And while the stumps of its legs

must buckle
and the elephant be brought
to its knees
in Honolulu where the sun shines every day

on natives in grass skirts
who invite the visitor from Cleveland to relax,
the Lunatic would have the elephant magnificently rise
above the crowd,

lamenting nothing, uttering one
triumphant cry after another
while unwinding over the condominiums like a thread of smoke,
as if to say, "I saw

and suffered what I saw"—in language unmistakable to us.

Trinity

The Lunatic remembers the three elephants best
withdrawn along the farthest stretch of their sanctuary,
somnambulists swinging their cumbersome trunks
flinging the history of human cruelty up into the air.

They seemed to know he was watching
but had settled on perpetual observation as something
to be brushed off, bending their brown heads,
confidential, as if in consultation about what to do next.

He thirsted for the trinity represented as them,
steering his binoculars slowly, as they moved slowly,
three in one, one too much, each leading his eye enviously
over the other, that knows what it knows, golden

with flung dust. So little time to search them out
for the secret hidden, in whose pocket,
whose lapel, before he moved on to the gazelles.

The Eternal Day

The first dawn that glowed out of the dark was the one sitting with my father in an idling Dodge along the edge of a field in early fall—the one waited for during pheasant season. We had driven far into those pastures, pulling onto the dirt road, the headlights shooting onto the hills like the insight of a ghost, neither of us saying much, the radio down low. Initially the ponderous movement from darkness to light, so faint one wasn't sure, if one thought about it—that crease of pink—then that bold forward thrust and that flush of cadmium yellow in the west, strove against the Dakota night dying quietly, quietly—then that curved, blood-red, imperially ascending leviathan of a sun that lit first the tops of the western bluffs, still only a radiance on the horizon which eventually took possession of the cornfields and the wheat fields, outdoing the sunflowers all facing east, like disciples. There were the cries of the first sparrows, detected clearly now since my father, out of respect for the dawn, had turned off the radio, then the crows, the windows rolled down to let the smoke from my father's cigar curl out, this first morning golden on the glittering leaves of corn soon to be harvested, everywhere that essential sanity of light, the dew so thick it soaked our pant legs when we walked through the blue gama grass before beginning a slow stalking up the corn rows, that movement with black night into dawn bestowing the feeling of some final absolution, as though with the sun we too had been reborn, which by the end of this day would have baked our arms red from resting elbows on the ledge of the car windows, fragrances of night different from the fragrances of dawn, exuded one doesn't know how. This was the first dawn, remembered the way one might remember, if one were a god, the day after mere creation.

On other mornings in bed listening to the flow from night to dawn and the screech of brakes from the garbage truck, not often, certainly often enough to recall, thunder rumbling in the disappearing night which sent me back to sleep, soft rain in its wake for awhile. Or only the sound of my father already out in the yard working his way down the hedgerow separating our yard from another's, clippers distantly clicking, my bowl of Cheerios before me, seeing the cobweb in the corner of the ceiling and wondering what that was—or pausing to whisper "photosynthesis" because we had been speaking about it in Science, contemplating how that process was possible, the mystery. And then the morning gone, the afternoon gone too, lost to the always turning world, the sprinklers left chittering in the dusk—that wetness clinging to the four o'clock flowers, the lolling irises and chrysanthemums, the snap-dragons that would slowly close round the honey bee pillaging that blossom for its sweetness.

The *tick tick tick* of the sprinkler heard without really listening, the *swoosh* that spread its hushed spray at one's bare feet before the great swaying away, the cottonwoods in the backyard dripping and gleaming after the sprinkler passed through their leaves, until my satisfied father appeared from the side door to stand awhile, suddenly thoughtful, sating himself on the delicious sorrow of a dark blue moon, lifting high over Riverview Avenue, and adjacent to that moon the first star asserting itself in a pale sky above Bonnie

Robinson's apron, turning first one flower then another. The squeak of the spigot twisted clockwise, then counter-clockwise (the years had not taught the mind, and never would, which was which to switch the sprinkler off, the sprinkler on) mingled with the *coo* of the mourning dove, so melancholy, the crickets along the edges of the clipped hedge singing, the aroma of my father's pipe smoke in the diffident breeze coming and going.

    After night had arrived (a screen door pulled on its spring), through the innumerable living room windows the flickering screens of black and white televisions: Connie Tinker shouting out to her son Bobbie—once, twice—the streetlights sputtering on, the day vanished, gone no one knows where, somewhere surely—elsewhere. And the moths enacted their mad dance as though *ad infinitum* around the green lamp on the back porch flicked on at twlight, and negligently left burning through till sunrise.

September Elegy for My Mother

So there lies my mother
in the profound pose of the dead,
capable only of one emotion.
I put my hand on her forehead.
Her eyes are closed.
Where now is that woman?
And I remember her knuckles
in the light of that modest yellow bulb
of her Singer sewing machine,
sliding blue denim underneath
the stuttering needle.
Remember too her sleep
when she leaned away
from reading *Of Time and the River,*
lips parted, there in her blue velvet chair
beside the white latticed window.
My mother's presence has become
the absence of *there*. For her
no more *there*—none.
I touch those clasped arthritic hands,
her mouth a crease.
One final unsatisfying stare
at my mother who walked
the golden wind-blown leaves with me,

wind in her brown hair,
pressed her cheek against my forehead,
dismissed me, called me back.
One more fierce look before they
load her away—away!—
never asking me again,
there, in terror: *Why are you so late?*
Where have you been?

Pet Shop

The ribbon snake holds so still
it doesn't exist. Same goes for the iguana.

Koi and goldfish drift in languorous bliss.
The white rat scratches urgently behind its left ear.

DON'T TEASE THE BIRDS shouts the cardboard sign
in red highlighter. The disinterested teenage in purple sandals

saunters off, running his crimson-ringed middle finger
over the lovebird's neck, leaving behind the boa

behind a dish, the terrified eye of the lizard so intent
it could be Iscariot. Why seek analogies

for what just is what it is?
My immediate task is to find a treat for my cat

but I get distracted watching white mice
lounging like concubines

one on top of the other, their feet extremely pink,
their eyes pink as their feet. Who wouldn't want

to take the parrot home and hear it repeat?
Who wouldn't want the boa coiled

round one's neck, to caress the Mongolian gerbil's
soft curved back? The lizard blinks.

Goldfish rise effortlessly, dart and flash,
ejecting a curlicue of feces that lifts end over end.

Nothing's like anything the cockatoo screams
from its pedestal, potentate of all this.

I turn back past the kid
at the cash register, just as the boa constrictor oozes out,

unraveling like the mind of a molester,
searching for one true thing.

GETTING THE CHRISTMAS TREE TO LEAVE

I have dragged the Christmas tree out of the house,
leaving a trail of needles in her wake. Now,
a star of tin foil on her brow,
she belies what came to her last week
when I wrapped her in a gown
and strung her with momentary lights.
Is this the belle of the ball who told
the juiciest stories, legs spread on the sofa, chain-smoking,
who make a spectacle of herself sipping martinis
and who gave her number to everyone,
growing drunker and drunker,
teasing the older men with kisses
blown from the palm of her delectable hand?
Is this the girl we all acted like morons for?
Let her sleep it off now in the cold,
covered in her innocence in this blanket of falling snow.

CLARINET

My father took it out on Sunday,
squinting up to the mouthpiece
while screwing it on tight, the reed
licked until it was damp,
after which he'd flutter up and down
the scales while sitting
on the edge of his old brown ottoman.
Clarinet lifted slightly then,
back straight, eyes askance
at sheet music on the stand,
turning it deftly with his hand,
I would see him there in passing
on my way to the bathroom,
not paying much attention
except when a run of notes so elegant
they broke my heart began.
And never seemed to end.
I'd pause, listen, the clear high riffs
coming from him
who couldn't carry a tune,
although my father liked to dance,
the two of them together
in that sunlit den saying *Yes*
to something I couldn't

quite fathom, this life
perhaps with its starched white shirts drying
on the line, mowed grass,
daughters whispering in bed.
Death, never mentioned in our house,
brought a stop to that.
My father was buried with his alto clarinet,
he all ash, it unassembled, black.

Missouri

Now it is merely a river of the mind
veiled in soft mysterious fog,
and yet in the mind commensurate
with everything revealed, everything imagined,
far pelicans in pairs at dusk, familial,

the force of water against a white-washed prow.
And more than the mind allowed,
stars clustering, the moon a scimitar,
and looping blue swallows with one pleasing delinquent
red-winged blackbird piercing the warm

night air. And gnats—gnats everywhere.
I am beguiled again by the mind's
capacity to remember such harrowing
of sky and windless silhouettes,
bronzed river water flowing, now as then.

Little Dipper

Those stars are mine tonight. Whatever you want for yourself
(meteors fainting, crossing satellites)...they are yours.
But let that Little Dipper I could not find as child
belong to me, walking with my investigating canine

out to the mailbox on the dark drive. Oh and that ethereal
once-in-a-blue moon above the subdivision--I'll take that too assigned
somewhere in the heart
that has thumped through terrors and disappointments

along with love. They mattered. They do not matter now.
Strange how what I obsessed so much about no longer crosses
my mind: "I love you. I loved you." I leave you now
with these unintelligible lyrics that have everything to do with rowing

a silver boat at first light through reeds with the sun shining down
on green water.
It makes me happy to be here with my dog.
He strains. He wants to walk on. And why not.

This is what you desired, is it not?--to your surprise
the nomenclature of constellations
primordial as a snake swallowing a goat from behind. And the ease
of setting everything aside. And those seven stars all mine.

Why Men Don't Write About Their Wives

It took a lifetime for the Lunatic to figure out
he hadn't the slightest idea
who she was. Reading John Milton's *Paradise Lost*
one night, he elected to set things right. He would recall
what had never dawned on him

in an epithalamion of all their vows,
her face as monosyllabic and drawn and haunted now
as that which miraculously appeared
to Milton in his sonnet "Methought I Saw." He'd been blind
and completely missed what she'd put up with for so long,

his Dominican cigar smoke stinking up the whole house
composing his righteous diatribes, his holding court
on everything from Boccaccio to the state of the art.
Hadn't she once confessed to him
when they were courting, cuddled in his loft

with the fire down to a hush, she had waited all of her life
to be touched like this? Three days the Lunatic labored over his encomium
—a litany of *faux pas*—until he had to admit he could not get
it right, this catalogue which kept coming up
against forgetting absolutely everything from the start.

FROM
THE DOUBLE GENESIS

Serpens Nebula

Look at the universe
in a photograph and you
begin to brood. Blessed
are the angels that pass it
all off with a laugh.
Their uninterest in stars
is a source of great
comfort to me. What,
after all, will we say
when that mystery pours through our hearts?

ABOUT THE AUTHOR

Dennis Sampson was born and raised in South Dakota. His seven volumes of poetry include *The Double Genesis, Forgiveness, Constant Longing, Needlegrass,* and *For my Father Falling Asleep at Saint Mary's Hospital, Within the Shadow of a Man,* and *The Lunatic in the Trees.* The recipient of grants from The Virginia Council on the Arts and The North Carolina Arts Council, Sampson's poems have appeared in such magazines as *The American Scholar, The Ohio Review, The Hudson Review* and many others. He has taught as Writer-in-Residence at Sweet Briar College in Virginia, as the Visiting Poet in the M.F.A Program in Creative Writing at UNC Wilmington, and at Wake Forest University.

www.ingramcontent.com/pod-product-compliance
Lightning Source LLC
Chambersburg PA
CBHW030111100526
44591CB00009B/359